WANCHO SCRIPT

T0078208

WANCHO SCRIPT

First Publication

2013

BANWANG LOSU

Partridge books may be ordered through booksellers or by contacting:

Partridge India
Penguin Books India Pvt.Ltd
11, Community Centre, Panchsheel Park, New Delhi 110017
India
www.partridgepublishing.com
Phone: 000.800.10062.62

Dedicated to Wanchonu
And my mother

Saying;
"Behind every successful man there is a woman"

It is true for me, behind this book publication there is a great role of my mother, inspite of all hardship, she encouraged me to get education even in the absence of father, and she is super-human for me.

On the other hand, the Wanchonu, who has let me, to think over the script as per the need of hour.

PRAYER

ᒡᒐᒕᒪᒪ ᏮᏮ

ᒆ' ᒡᒐᒕᒪᒪ ᒥᒕᒆ

ᒆᒆᏮᒕᒆᏃ ᒡᒪᒪ ᔛᒕᒆᏰ Ꮻᒕᒆ

ᒧᒥ Ꮻᒕᒆ ᔛᒕᒆᏰ Ꮻᒕᒆ

ᒪᒐᒐ Ꮻᒕᒆ ᒆᒕᒧ Ꮻᒕᒆ ᒧᒕᒆᏃ

ᒐᒪᒪ Ꮻᒕᒆ ᒡᒆᒆ Ꮻᒕᒆ ᒧᒕᒆᏃ

ᒪᒐ ᒥᒕᒆ ᔛᏮ ᒎᒕᒆᏃ Ꮻᒕᒆ

Ꮾᒒ ᒆᒕᒆᏃ ᒧᒪᒆᒕ Ꮻᒕᒆ

ᒡᏰᒆᔛᏰ ᒡᒐᒕᒪᒪ

ᏫᏰᔛᒪᏰᒆ ᒆᒎᒆᏫᒆᏃ

Acknowledgements

In 2001, when I was in class XI, decided to write on the topic 'Socio-Economics of Wanchos' initiated by S.V.K. Chandran, ST Economics, who formed a team and started collection of materials. Later, when I tried on it to translate into Wancho Language using Roman Script, I was surprised to find out the complexity of our language which was unable to write using Roman Script. Since then, I started a research on sounds (Phonetics) of Wancho language and represented them with symbols. But, at that time, I had no idea at all regarding script finding.

I found some unique and strange sound(s) which are not familiar to Hindi and English languages. I collected such sounds separately from the common sounds, of which most of the sounds are familiar to Hindi, some of them were very peculiar. It was also not so easy to designed symbols that would be simple, memorable and easy to learn, smooth and fast while writing. I designed both capital and small letters in the first try, later I found technical problem when I put them on the computer keyboard which is designed according to 26 letter of English Alphabet (small + capital = 52 letters), and we have 42 letters (42 x 2 = 84 or 42 + 42 = 84) which is not easy to fit in the keyboard so I deleted small letters. Hindi has no small letters but it has matras (capital + matras = 104 or full-sound + half-sound = 104) approx. hence, typing Hindi in computer keyboard is not an easy task.

My pace was very slow at the beginning of 2007. Since, the mid of 2007 when I received a letter from Mr. Nokkai Wangsaham regarding the Workshop on 'Endangered Wancho Language' since that day, I worked day and night without sleep to present my research paper.

But, in that workshop the intention/motto of organizing team was to work with Roman Script and moreover, my preparation was not convincing as I had wished due to shortage of time. Hence, my presentation was not successful. However, I have got lot of appreciation, inspiration, aspiration and encouragement from many people especially Mr. Mankai Wangsu(Wancho Bible Translator), and the a person with whom I met and discussed on my work they supported. I would mention their names in particular, Mr. D.S. Parmar, S.V.K. Chandran, and Hare Krishna Sharma, Miss Asha Yongam who guided Hindi Articulation, my brothers who never let me feel lonely and Mr. Jatwang Wangsa (who played active role in every possible assistance), and many more.

My gratitude goes to Mr. Namjang Wangsu (ADC, Longding) who gave me assurance to initiate seminar with ecstatic manner in first meet. Mr. N.Longhi Naam (CO,Khonsa), Mr. Naiphu Wangsu (ADO,Khonsa), Mr.Manpa Wangsu(ADO,Khonsa), Mr. Ngamwang Wangham(ST, Longding), Mr. Ahua Wangsu (Dist.Coach), Mr. Bolam Boham (ADEO), Mr. Sompha Wangpan, Dr. Manlong Ralongham, Mr. Sompho Wangsa, Mr. Nefa Wangsa and many friends who attended the 1st ever Seminar on Wancho Script held on 28th-29th April 2012 in HQ. Longding, under the Chairmanship of Ex-Minister Shri. Hejam Ponglaham. The Seminar was organized by the Wancho Students' Union, President Mr. Manphua Wangsu, Gen. Secy. Mr. Pholem Wangnow and the Wancho Cultural Society President Mr. Gangdiap Gangsa, Gen.Secy. Mr. Nokkai Wangsaham, and their associate members.

Apart from that, I thank Changwang Wangsu, Tonlong Rangkham, Honrang Maham and Ngatong Gangsa for adding four more sounds in the script, these are 𝒮, 𝒮, 𝒮 and 𝒮 respectively.

It would remain incomplete if I did not thank Mr. Honchun Ngandam (Hon'ble MLA, 60th Pongchau-Wakka Assembly Constituency; Cum- Parliamentary Secretary Horticulture) A.P, Mr. Thangwang Wangham (Hon'ble MLA, 59th Longding-Pamou; Parliamentary Secretary, IPR&P) A.P. and Mr. Newlai Tingkhatra (Hon'ble Minister, WRD & SW), Arunachal Pradesh and the Wanchonu for their immense help and contributions in publication of this book. Because of them, I have got an ample opportunity to work on the Script. I hope the Wanchonu will welcome my work, because this is the Identity and permanent Property of the Wanchos.

I would also thank Mr. Wangdan Wangpan and his co-workers Mr. Rabindra Kumar Bhagat, Kanishka Kumari, Shanjo Jami, and Neerav Doshi for excellent job in making cartoon animation film in Wancho style and language. And, especial thank to the Secretary of Governor & Planning, Govt. of Arunachal Pradesh, Shri. Ankur Garg (IAS) for his inspiring message on the Wancho Script. I also thank Mr. Dipangkar Baruah, who made the software (Typeface) of Wancho Script.

Last but not the least, I would like to thank Dr. Vineeta Dowerah, Assistant Professor of English, in Wangcha Raj Kumar Govt. College, Deomali, and Miss Phejon Wangsa of Kamhua Noknu village, who edited the manuscript more accurately and grammatically with using apt words which added flavor in the sentences.

Minister
WRD, WCD,
Arunachal Pradesh
0360-2291365(o)
0360-2292419 (f)
09436040017

Message

I am pleased to know that the first ever a book on "The Wancho Script" is being published by Shri Banwang Losu, a Wancho research scholar from Longding shortly.

Newlai Tingkhatra

The Wancho tribe is a recognized tribe and has a sizeable population inhabits in districts of Longding and Tirap and speaks a living language "Wancho".

There is plethora of folk tale and folk lore is prevalent and spoken in the community, but no attempt has so far been made to compile or codify the language in written form owing to non-devising of the Wancho Script. These are the treasure trove of the Wancho community required to be preserved in the written form for posterity of future generations.

To me, language development is the series of ongoing planned actions that a language community needs to ensure that its language continues to flourish and serve its changing social, cultural, economic, and spiritual needs and goals. It may be supported by several writing systems based on historic, political, educational, or other reasons. A grave concern for many in the world is the large number of minority languages that are endangered or at risk of extinction. Every language has inherent value, and that speakers of minority languages should have the tools and techniques available to project and enhance their cultural and linguistic heritage.

This is a gigantic task; the research scholar has in hand. I hope that developers of this project will consider the differences between scripting and system programming and choose the most powerful tool for each task.

I wish success to the Wancho language developers in their endeavour.

Newlai Tingkhatra

MLA, 60th
Pongchau-wakka
Assembly Constituency
Arunachal Pradesh

Message

I am proud of having our own independent Script like other civilized society; it is beyond gravity to appreciate the author Mr. Banwang Losu who worked hard since last twelve years. I was informed and shown his marvelous work in 2007, since then I began supporting him morally. Now time has come to support him from every possible angles; morally, physically, mentally and financially.

(Honchun Ngandam)

I am very serious and honest in the matter of culture and traditions of Wancho since my schooling days taking active role in various social activities. In the field of literature too I have attempted many a times to preserve our useful and important ideas learned from our forefathers. Wancho Grammar published in 2009 is an example of my contribution with Fr. Francis T.J.Sdb. Education is an inseparable element for human beings which started since the conception in mother's womb till the last breathe, in short 'Womb to Tomb'. So education in mother tongue is more easier and effective for children as he or she has started learning in their mother's womb.

Our culture is very defined and rich which contain the value of moral life, now it is diminishing due to lack of systematic, scientific and value added teaching. If we want to live a civilized life we have to recall the past rich culture with modern scientific attitude, for this purpose we need to preserve the history and past information in written form or printed books using our own script which could hold accurate or exact sounds and pronunciations without losing meaning and pronunciation unlike Hindi and English. Therefore, I honestly welcome the new energetic youths to come up with good hope to bring Wanchonu towards development and pride.

Honchun Ngandam, MLA
Parliamentary Secy. Horti.

MLA Cottage No. 10
Itanagar, A.P.
Date : 14.10.2012

Message

**(Thangwang
Wangham)**

If language is the gateway to human evolution, script is the means to sustain it. Language is the essence of cultural identity. Language embodies a value system to relate to our own identity and root. Today, like many other languages of the world, Wancho language is also susceptible to the onslaught of larger and powerful societies. Although, we have a very rich oral language, we urgently need a corresponding script that is native to us to preserve our culture and tradition to do justice to our posterity. Write language will not only help us in preserving our rich language but on the larger note, protect our culture in its original form from being swallowed up by other stronger cultures. So, the present generation has the responsibilities to evolve mechanism to protect and preserve our culture identity. And I sincerely hope that the development of script will play a major role in this direction.

I never have had such a pleasure while message for any other purpose as I am feeling now because it is a history in making. I salute initiative and effort of the people behind this novel idea.. I wish the Committee and other individuals who are burning midnight lamps to materialize the dreams of Wancho all success. I also commit my continued help in whatever form I can to promote and popularize the Wancho's Script in future.

Thangwang Wangham, MLA
Parliamentary Secy. *IPR&P*

Ankur Garg IAS
Secretary of Governor &
Secretary Planning
Govt. of Arunachal Pradesh

Raj Bhawan, Itanagar-791111
Ph. : +91-360-2212418
Fax : +91-360-2212508
garg_ankur@hotmail.com

Message

WANCHO LANGUAGE SCRIPT

Arunachal Pradesh is one of the most linguistically rich and diverse regions in the world, being home to twenty-six major tribes and more than hundred sub-tribes.

The vast majority of languages indigenous to Arunachal Pradesh belong to the Tibeto-Burman language family. The majority of these in turn belong to a single branch of Tibeto-Burman, namely Tani. While Monpa and Sherdukpen languages are spoken in the western part of the state, to the east of the Tani area lie three languages of the Mishmi group of Tibeto-Burman, i.e. Idu, Digaru and Miju. Further south, one finds the Singpho language, which is primarily spoken by large population in Myanmar. The Nocte and Wancho languages, which show affiliations to certain Naga languages, are spoken in the south eastern part of the State bordering Nagaland.

Some of the tribes already have written scripts for their languages. Having their own scripts helped those tribes to preserve their indigenous culture, faith, and traditions. It has also facilitated in maintaining strong roots to their heritage and encouraged use of their own language.

I am happy that Sh. Banwang Losu of the Wancho Community of Longding District is developing a script for Wancho language and hope that it will go a long way in preservation of the rich Wancho indigenous culture and values.

I commend all the members of Wancho community who are contributing with their efforts and wish them success in their endeavours.

Message

N.L. Naam
Circle Office

I am extremely delighted to know that Mr. B. Losu is introducing the first ever Wancho Script. It is really a matter of pride and marvelous work began by him which is on the corridor to mark a new chapter in the history of Wancho. This innovative and master piece of work done by him would definitely serve as an era of renaissance for the people of Wancho. At the very outset let me make clear to the readers that so far as English is concerned, it is an international language and it has been accepted as an official language in India also but, history reveals that great poets, novelist and writers of the world had came up with wonderful writings on their own language (Script) such as Rabindranath Tagor (Bengali Poet), Romain Rolland (French writer), Karl Max, Premchand (Hindi writer) etc. They wrote in their own languages, later their books have been translated in several of the languages. And now they are regarded as prominent figures in the field of literature.

As such, though a person may not feel perfect in others languages but the same person would be definitely comfortable enough to express views in own language. Thus, introducing of Wancho Script would help the aspirant writers, philosophers and thinkers especially from Wancho belt to become an excellent writer in their own language. It is absolutely true that one's identity is known by his/her language for example- in India Tamilian is known by Tamil, Kerelian by Malayalam, Orissa by Odiya, Assam by Assamese, Maharastra by Marathi, Punjab by Punjabi etc. Similarly, Wancho would be known by Wancho Laizi (Wancho Script).

I hope everyone would be interested to go through this newly published literature which will make you feel proude and ecstatic to have such a prestigious property among us. It will help to preserve our endangered rich cultural heritage enabling rest of the world to know who we are.

Nok Longhee Naam
Circle Officer

(xiv)

Message

It is a great privilege for me to extend my sincere thanks to Mr. B. Losu and greetings to the people of Wanchonu that, the creation of Longding District and introduction of Wancho Script is co-incident ever happened in the history of the development of Wancho Society. The history reveals that, Wancho is rich in her own heritage and culture by virtue of the existence in present inhabitation land.

Naiphu Wangsu
ADO, Khonsa

And it is our responsibillity to preserve, protect and promote our rich culture to keep our own identity in the eye of the other societies; therefore I welcome and encourage the new generation to come up with new innovative ideas to bring Wancho Society into the era of development and civilization.

Human has been known more intelligent than animal since man started learning language, and today we considered the society more civilized and developed who has written script other than verbal language. In spite of having civilized in various field since immemorial, today Wanchos are considered backward society due to absence of written script. Hence, every possible effort should be made to promote Wancho Script continuously from today onwards. Having independent Script is a matter of pride for our Community.

I also appeal the educated youth, leaders and well wishers of Wancho Community to come up with unity to bring this marvelous work successful even in national and international arena. And I am sure the people of Wancho are brave, straight forward towards progress and development.

Naiphu Wangsu
Agri. Development Officer
Khonsa

Message

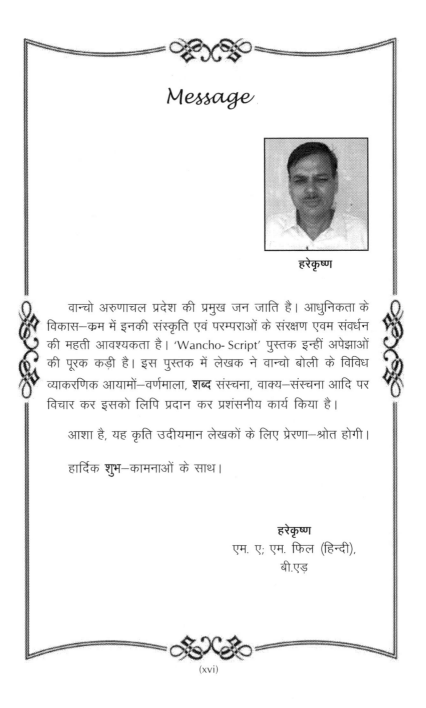

हरेकृष्ण

वान्चो अरुणाचल प्रदेश की प्रमुख जन जाति है। आधुनिकता के विकास–क्रम में इनकी संस्कृति एवं परम्पराओं के संरक्षण एवम संवर्धन की महती आवश्यकता है। 'Wancho- Script' पुस्तक इन्हीं अपेझाओं की पूरक कड़ी है। इस पुस्तक में लेखक ने वान्चो बोली के विविध व्याकरणिक आयामों–वर्णमाला, **शब्द** संरचना, वाक्य–संरचना आदि पर विचार कर इसको लिपि प्रदान कर प्रशंसनीय कार्य किया है।

आशा है, यह कृति उदीयमान लेखकों के लिए प्रेरणा–श्रोत होगी।

हार्दिक **शुभ**–कामनाओं के साथ।

हरेकृष्ण
एम. ए; एम. फिल (हिन्दी),
बी.एड़

Message

I feel extremely happy and proud to see that the first ever independent Wancho script has been developed and introduced in the Wancho Society through the sincere efforts and arduous tasks carried out by Mr. Banwang Losu. It will definitely help in preservation of this indigenous language which happens to be an important marker  of cultural identity of the people from being lost and in promoting the language for scholastic ventures.

The Wancho language is classified as the Naga group of Tibet-Burman branch. It has affinity with Nocte and Tangsa languages of the same language family. Linguistically, the Wanchos of Arunachal Pradesh are classified into three groups based on their dialectical differences- Upper Wancho(Tang group) inhabited in and around Pongchau and Wakka circle, Middle Wancho(Sang group) occupying Longding and Pumao circle, and Lower Wancho settled in the Kanubari circle of the district. Their language, commonly called 'Kah', differs mostly in terms of tone and pronunciation. Many people of the community converse in their link languages like Assamese and Hindi. The educated ones even speak in English. Under the influence and pressure of other dominant languages and culture, the Wanchos are facing difficulties in maintaining the link and continuity with their past. The non-availability of indigenous script has created difficulties for Wancho writers and the elite group to develop their language through literature. The vast treasure of indigenous language and relevant information is dying out without proper documentation. Their language, like many other indigenous languages of the world, may face a situation of endangerment. It was, of late, realized that their unique language would remain alive in its pure form if it can be documented with the help of a proper script.

The Wancho scholars opine that their language cannot be documented entirely by using Hindi or English alphabets (Devanagiri and Roman scripts respectively) as these alphabets cannot represent all the original sounds, tones and pronunciation of words of their language. It is not sufficient to transcribe the local language perfectly. The proposed modified Roman script, they believe, could not solve the script problem of the Wancho language and meet the immediate scholastic need of the literate and educated mass. There was an urgent need for common alphabets to document the existing language of the Wanchos with a uniform sound. Hence, it was felt that an independent Wancho script was required to transcribe different sounds that make different meaning. Thus, an independent Wancho script called 'Wancho Laizi' has been developed and introduced in the society. Lot of care has been taken to represent the existing sounds and tones.

I hope the people of the community will accept the script with pride and satisfaction and work for further development of their language and rich culture. I also hope to see the Wancho intellectuals use their own language and script for reflecting upon their thoughts and ideas and for understanding and remembering historical experiences, their cultural heritage, folks and the folk tradition. I expect the support and cooperation of the people in my present work related to the morphological and syntactical analysis of the Wancho language. At last, I wish them luck and extend congratulations to them on this noble achievement.

Dr. Vineeta Dowerah
M.A., Ph.D., PGCTE
Asst. Professor of English
Wangcha Rajkumar Govt. College
Deomali

PRONUNCIATION
डच्चारण शैली

Consonants			
IPA*Symbol	Usage	Hindi	Usage
P	cap/kæp/	प्	कैप्
b	rub/rʌb/	ब्	रब्
t	fit/fit/	ट्	फिट्
d	red/red/	ड्	रडे्
k	break/breik/	क्	ब्रक्
g	flag/flæg/	ग्	फलैग्
tʃ	rich/nʃ/	च्	रिच्
dʒ	badge/bædʒ/	ज्	बेज्
f	life/laif/	फ़्	लाइफ़्
v	wave/werv/	व्	वेव्
θ	myth/miθ/	थ्	मिथ्
ð	bath θ/b θið/	द्	बेद्
s	fuss/fʌs/	स्	फस
z	railings/railiŋz/	ज्	रेलिङ्ज्
ʃ	fish/fiʃ/	श्	फिश्
ʒ	vision/viʒn/	श्	व़िान
h	hat/hæt/	ह	हैट्
m	fame/feim/	म्	फ़्रेम
n	fin/fin/	न्	फिन
ŋ	ring/nŋ/	ड्	रिङ
l	file/fail/	ल्	फ़ाइल
r	run/rʌn/	र	रन्
(r)	for/fo:(r)/	र्	फ़ॉ(र्)
j	granular/grænj θθ(r)/	य	ग्रैन्यल(र्)
w	won/wʌn/	व	वन्

(xix)

Vowels and Dipthongs

I	fig/fig/	इ / ि	फिग्
i:	see/si:/	ई / ी	सी
e	ten/ten/	ए / ॆ	टॆन्
æ	cat/kæt/	ऐ / ै	कैट्
a:	far/fa:(r)/	आ / ा	फ़ार्
ɒ	lot/lɒt/	ऑ / ॉ	लॉट्
ɒ̃	croissant/krwæsɒ̃/	आ / ँ	क्रवैसॉं
ɔ:	saw/sɔ:/	ऑ / ॉ	.सॉ
ʊ	put/pʊt/	उ / ु	पुट्
u	actual/ækt ʃuəl/	उ / ु	ऐक्चुअल्
u:	too/tu:/	ऊ / ू	टू
ʌ	cut/kʌt/	अ	कट्
3:	birt/b3:d/	अ	बड्
ə	about, paper/ ə'baut; 'peɪpe(r)/	अ	अ'बाउट्; ''पेप(र्)
eɪ	fade/feld/	एॆ	फ़ेड्
əʊ	go/gʊe/	ओ / ो	गो
aɪ	five/faiv/	आ + इ / ा + इ	फ़ाइव्
ɔɪ	boy/bɔɪ/	ऑ + इ/ॉ + इ	बॉइ
aʊ	now/naʊ/	आ + उ/ा + उ	नाउ
ɪə	near/nɪə(r)/	इ + अ/ि + अ	निअ(र्)
eə	chair/t ʃeə(r)/	ए + अ/ॆ + अ	चेअर्
ʊə	pure/pjʊə(r)/	उ + अ/ु + अ	प्युअर्

Ref : Oxford English-English Hindi Dictionary (editors - Dr. Suresh Kumar & Dr. Ramanath Sahai) Published in india by Oxford University Press - 23rd impression June 2012.

INTERNATIONAL PHONETICS (IPA) SYMBOLS

a   Back open unrounded vowel used (Eng. [a] in car)

b   voice bilabial plosive (Eng. [b] in labour)

tʃ   voiceless palato-alveolar affricate (Eng. [ch] in church)

d   voiced alveolar plosive (Eng. [d] in lady)

g   voiceless velar plosive (Eng.[g] in ago)

j   voiced unrounded palatal semi vowel (Eng. [y] in you)

l   voiced alveolar lateral (Eng. [l] in love)

n   voiced alveolar nasal (Eng. [n] in no)

p   voiceless bilabial plosive (Eng. [p] in pea)

t   voiceless alveolar plosive (Eng. [t] in tea)

θ   voiceless dental fricative (Eng. [th] in thing)

f   voiceless labio-dental fricative (Eng. [f] in four)

ɫ   vioceless retroflex lateral fricative (Hand in Khasa)

S   voiceless alveolar fricative (Eng. [s] in see)

ts   voiceless alveolar affricative (In Wancho [Tsai] meaning; song)

ʒ   voiced palato-alveolar fricative (Eng. [s] in measure)

W   voiced rounded labio-velar semi-vowel (Eng. [w] in we)

V   voiced labio-dental fricative (Eng. [v] in ever)

K   voiceless velar plosive (Eng. [c] in car)

o   Back open rounded vowel

ɔ: Back open rounded vowel

r   voiced post-alveolar frictionless continuant (Eng. [r] in red)

m   voiced bilabial nasal (Eng. [m] in me)

x   voiceless velar fricative (as [kh] in khaki)

H   voiceless Epiglottal fricative (Eng. [H] in house)

æ   Font unrounded vowel between half-open and open positions (Eng. [æ] in **Ae**roplane

i   Front unrounded vowel between close and half-close positions (Eng. [i] in in

ŋ   Voiced velar nasal (Eng. [ng] in sing

oŋ   back closed rounded vowel (Eng. [oŋ/ong] in long

ɲ   Voiced palatal nasal

ʡ or ʔ   Epiglottal & glottal stop

CONTENTS

1 INTRODUCTION

This book aims at the preservation and prevention of the Wancho language from being lost and at keeping the identity of the Wanchos alive and intact, as well as, at the development of the Wancho Society like other developed cultures through the introduction of script especially in the field of knowledge through education. The language of Wancho, in my opinion, is authentic and accurate but I am not averred on it if somebody finds some mistakes. Sounds are recorded in CD-disc (Cartoon Animation Film) given along with this book which will guide/help in the production of sounds with the presentation of symbols. Symbols are designed in a simple style so that it is easier to understand. It appears smooth and occupies less space while writing.

The Wancho languages vary slightly from one village to another as it falls under the **largest linguistic group** in the eastern Arunachal Pradesh. It can be written in one's own language and pronunciation. The Alphabet introduced and published for the first time may look strange and new to everybody. It might also appear difficult to understand in the beginning. But, in reality, it is very easy and simple. Only a little effort is required. Pedagogically, there might occur some deficiency in performance skills due to inadequate rehearsal and insufficient teaching-learning materials. In spite of such limitations, I have worked hard to make it easy and effective.

This script and language may spread to wider horizons in near future benefiting some parts of Arunachal Pradesh and Nagaland, border areas of Myanmar, Bhutan and some parts of even North-East-region and other countries as well because it belongs to the great Tibeto-Burman family of Languages according to Shafer, Benedict Egerod and Voegelin's works on the classification of languages. This book shall not remain confined to the Wancho community alone, but shall be of immense help and utility to any language lover across the globe. It took twelve years for me to complete this work with the constant support and inspiration from my friends.

I have got comments from many in the 1st phase seminar regarding the possession of a common language. We already have a common language since time immemorial. What you speak and I understand is called a common language. There might be slight differences between the two but they are not strange to each other at all. We cannot ignore any language considering a particular language as the superior language and suppressing others as subordinate or sub standard ones. Such a blunder or misconception about languages may lead to the extinction of mass language and will diminish the motto of having a script of the language .

I am giving few examples of English language which is formed by mixing many languages, say- **HAPPY:** meaning content, pleased, glad, joyful, cheerful, and blissful, etc. **SAD:** means depressing, gloomy, miserable, cheerless, heartbreaking, distressing, heartrending and poignant. **MERCY:** means compassion, pity, clemency, forgiveness, kindness, sympathy, understanding, leniency etc. **All these words are taken from Greek, Latin, Hebrew, French etc. which became a common language, i.e. English language.**

In Hindi, the word **MOUNTAIN** has different names as- पर्वत, पहाड़, गिरी और हिम; **SKY:** आकाश, आसमान, अम्बर, व्योम, गगन; **LOVE:** प्यार, प्रेम, मुहब्बत, इश्क and so on.

All these words come from Urdu, Sanskrit, Bhojpuri, Bengali, Gujarati, etc. Similarly, Wanchos have different names (Synonyms) of one thing say, **SKY-** *Gang* in upper Wancho area, *Jang/Zang* in middle, and *Rang* in the Lower belt. Similarly, **SONG** is called *Tai, Tsai, Son, Lailung, Boa*; **SOIL** as *Kah, Hah, Chah*; **CLOTH** as *Khu, Khat, Nee,* etc.

Every language is equally important as it has its own value, taste, beauty and a knowledge system. Hence, every language of Wancho (From Konsa to Kannubari) will be included as a common language of Wancho Society. At the same time, the people of the community should try and learn each other's language so that it brings the spirit of oneness, togetherness, unity and social harmony among the Community.

Script is only the collection of sound or sounds with symbolic presentation of a particular language which can hold different kind of sounds spoken by human in a particular community or society. It acts like a mobile phone. For example, a mobile phone receives voice spoken by you. The spoken words may either be in English, Hindi, Japanese, and Chinese, Hebrew or any other languages of the world.

The cell phone transmits the same language used by the speaker to the receiver. Similarly, Wancho script can hold your language no matter whether you belong to the upper belt, middle belt, the lower belt or other community. The collected sounds can produce uncountable languages just as the six strings of a guitar which produces uncountable different kinds of tones or notes. You can write what you speak.

Having Independent script is like having third eye in a finger tip which enables us to see another world, which may either be the day or the night. It may also be the past, present or the future as shown in figure-1, 2 & 3, respectively. The Wancho linguisticians, philosophers & phoneticians are welcome if there is something to be edited, clarified and modified because it is the first time that we are introducing/developing such symbols and sounds for reaching a common linguistic platform.

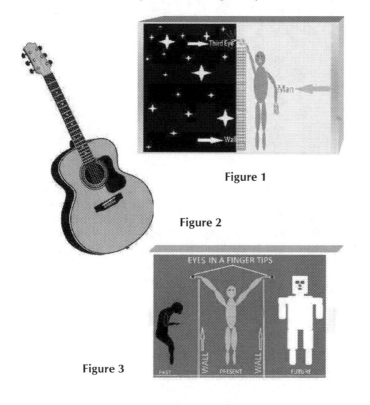

Figure 1

Figure 2

Figure 3

2 LANGUAGE

Language is the 'species-specific' and 'species-uniform'possession of man. It is god's special gift to mankind. Without language human civilization, as we now know it, would have remained impossibility. Language is ubiquitous. It is present everywhere- in our thoughts and dreams, prayers and meditations, relations and communications, and sanskars and rituals.

Besides being a means of communication, and store house of knowledge, it is an instrument of thinking as well as source of delight (eg. singing). Language dissipates superfluous nervous energy, directs motion in others, both man and animals, sets matter in motion as in charms and incantations, transfers knowledge from one person to another and from one generation to another.

Language is also the maker or unmaker of human relationships. It is the use of language that makes life bitter or sweet. Without language man would have remained only a dumb animal. It is our ability to communicate through words that makes us different from animals. Because of its omnipresence language is often taken for granted. But many a time it has become the serious concern not only of linguisticians but also of philosophers, logicians, psychologists, scientists and literary critics.

Whereas 'language' in the abstract is our faculty to speak; or 'the faculty of speech, which all human beings hold in common'; 'a language' is 'a particular code, a set of conversations which we operate through the possession of the faculty of speech;and language is not held in common by all human beings but only by those who belong to specific-community'.

Since linguistics is the study of language, it is imperative for a linguist to know what language is. Language is a very complex human phenomenon; all attempts to define it have proved inadequate. In a nut shell, language is an 'organized noise' used in actual social situations. That is why it has also been defined as 'contextualized systematic sounds'.

The continuance of a foreign language decreases the value of originality and independent thinking and secondly it is not the language of the majority but of the minority. Language must be the language of the people and for the people. Original ideas are to be inspired and the culture and traditions of the Wancho are to be honored, our language is a simple language which can be written and understood after little efforts. Many centuries back, our ancestors used rocks, pillars and parchment with a view to recording and perpetuating their most important thoughts and achievements in the language they then understood.

Mankind's most valuable treasure of thoughts is carefully preserved in the golden casket of books. All this rich source of knowledge, inspiration and guidance is within the easy reach of those who care to be a little hardworking and studies and how understood the methods which yield the rich harvest of fruitful ideas.

According to ancient linguist of India, Patanjali, language is that human expression which is uttered out by speech organs. In the encyclopedia Britannica, Vol. 13, language is defined as "a system of conventional, spoken or written symbols by means of which human beings, as members of a social group and participants of its culture, communicate." Some other definitions which are currently popular in linguistic circle are cited below:-

* "Language is a primarily human and non-instinctive method of communicating ideas, emotions and desires by means of a system of voluntarily produced symbols."
  .

* "A system of communication by sound, i.e. through the organs of speech and hearing, among human beings of a certain group or community, using vocal symbols possessing arbitrary conventional meanings."   .

* According to Transformational Generative linguists like Noam Chomsky, language is the innate capacity of native speakers to understand and form grammatical sentences.   .

* Anthropologist regard language as a form of cultural behavior, sociologists as an interaction   between members of social group, students of   literature as an artistic medium, philosophers as a means of interpreting human experience, language teachers as a

set of skills.

Truly, language is such a complex phenomenon that to define it in terms of a single level as knowledge, behavior, skill, habit, an event or an object, cannot solve the problem of its definition. None of the above definitions are perfect. Each of them just hints at certain characteristics of language. Hence instead of defining language, it would be worthwhile to understand its major characteristics.   .

Stephen Hawking quoted in his famous book 'The Universe in a Nutshell':

"About six or eight thousand years ago, a major new development occurred. We developed written language. This meant that information could be passed from one generation to the next without having to wait for the very slow process of random mutations and natural selection to code it into the DNA sequence. The amount of complexity increased enormously.

A single paperback romance could hold as much information as the difference in DNA between apes and humans, and a thirty-volume encyclopedia could describe the entire sequence of human DNA.

Even more important, the information in books can be updated rapidly. The current rate at which human DNA is being updated by biological evolution is about one bit a year. But there are two hundred thousand new books published each year, a new-information rate of over million bits a second. Only one bit in a million is useful, that is still a hundred thousand times faster than biological evolution. This transmission of data through external, non-biological means has led the human race to dominate the world".

These lines described that how important the invention of script is. Which impact to the human evolution and civilization in the field of knowledge, science and technology especially through writings and publication of books. So, written language is far more important and powerful than verbal languages.

Stephen Hawking, Professor of Mathematics in Cambridge University who wrote the inspiring sequel to A Brief History of Time and winner of the 2002 Aventis Prizes for Science Books.

Ref. Linguistics & Phonetics, Edition-2005-06. P-1 &2 for language section.

3 THE WANCHOS

The Wanchos are one of the major indigenous tribes inhabited in the Longding district of Arunachal Pradesh. This newly created district is the divine abode of the warm- hearted tribe known in the ancient history as 'head- hunters', who have preserved their own ethos, traditional heritage, enriched culture, time tested ethical treasure of immense values and a strong social fabric. The Wanchos posses immaculate virtues like open heartedness, fellow feelings free from ego, honesty and purity of mind. They are straight- forward in their outlook, fearless by nature, adventurous in spirit and pious by nature.

The land of this pristine tribe extends from 26 degree 30' north to 27 degree 16' North Latitude and 95 degrees 16' east to 95 degree 20' east Longitude. The Wanchos inhabit around 1062 Sq.Kms, which covers 45 percent of the total area of Tirap District. This fascinating tribe lives within the periphery of Patkai Range of the Himalayas ranging from 200 metres to 2000 metres above sea level. The Wancho land- sacred land of "Rising Sun"- is in divine providence with various natural vegetations, lush green flora, and wide range of fauna, high mountain peaks, picturesque landscapes, mind boggling scenic beauty, gushing rivers and unfathomable natural resources.

The tribe has been dwelling in their present habitat from the time immemorial and they are believed to have migrated from China to Myanmar, then to two places, namely, Tangnu and Tsangnu of Twinsang district of Nagaland. Due to some domestic disputes they had again migrated to the present habitation. Wancho valley is situated to the east of India at the international border with Myanmar to the south, Assam to the north, Koinyak (Nagaland state) to the South west, and Nocte tribe in the north east. There are 67 villages, 51,022 populations (Male 26,447 & Female 24,575) with the average literacy rate of 25.36 percent (Male 35.28%, Female 14.20%). As per popullation census 2001.

This socio- culturally rich tribe does not have a script to use/ document their language into a written form. As we know that language is the organization of sounds, of vocal symbols which is very essential in human life to express/communicate the external and internal feelings of a person to another, and for transferring the history/information/ traditional knowledge, etc. from one generation to the next generations. In this connection only the verbal communication is not sufficient to preserve its knowledge system.   .   .

As a result, so many useful information and remarkable happenings of the past have got lost or erased from the memories of the folk and it can never be recalled accurately or never at all due to the absence of script. Hence it is high time we understand that the language of Wanchos is in the verge of endangerment now. We fear to lose the original sounds, voices, words and its meanings if it is not stored in a written form. More specifically, it is not appreciable and inevitable to keep the language documented in written form by using English (Roman) or Hindi (Devanagiri) alphabets because English and Hindi alphabets cannot sufficiently pickup the original sounds and pronunciations of the Wancho language.

Keeping this problem in mind, I have invented the 'Wancho Alphabet and Counting Numbers/ numerals' to preserve the endangered language of this age old tribe. The Wancho alphabet consists of 42 speech sounds **(29 consonants and 13 vowels)** and numerals from 0 to 9 digits respectively. Each letter produces different sounds; some of the letters produces very unique sounds which cannot be written or transcribed in English or Hindi.

The Wancho Alphabet has not been plagiarized from others' script. It has its own independent symbols, except zero (cipher) in numeral. The letters are arranged systematically which begins with letter '𑊂' / **a,** आ / and ends with letter '𑋁 𑋁' (yih) as shown in the next pages. Some of the letters represent human action, appearance of animals, birds, plants, tools, furniture and tattoos etc.

4 LAIZI or LAILI
(A L P H A B E T)

VOWELS - 13

𝞗, 𝑇, 𝑇, 𝟃, 𝟤, 𝟄, 𝟨, 𝟫,

𝞐, 𝟕, 𝟗, 𝟨 and 𝟨

CONSONANTS - 19

𝟨, 𝟨, 𝟨, 𝟨, 𝟨, 𝟰, ⟍, ⟋, 𝟨,

𝟨, 𝟰, ⇀, 𝘕, 𝟨, 𝟨, 𝟨, 𝟨, 𝟨,

𝟨, 𝟰, 𝟨, 𝟨, 𝟨, 𝟨, 𝟨, 𝟨, 𝟨,

𝟨 and 𝟰

UNIQUENESS IN SOUNDS
VOWELS & CONSONANTS - 12

𝘕, 𝟨, 𝟨, 𝟨, 𝟨, 𝟫, 𝞐, 𝟕, 𝟗,

𝟨, 𝟨 and 𝟰

KEYBOARD ACCESS CHART

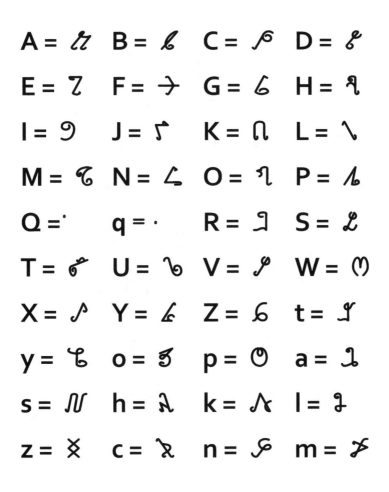

'✗' is a symbol of Wancho design use in Galeys, Bags, Coats, Necklaces, Belts, and Crafts etc.

KEYBOARD ACCESS
CHART

'~, !, @, #, $ = 𝒫, %, ^
= ÷ , &, * = ×, (), - = 🕊,
+, =, :, ;, " ' <, >, .,
?, /

1 = ໂ   2 = 9

3 = Ҩ   4 = ♪

5 = ♪   6 = ?

7 = V   8 = ƒ

9 = ☇   0 = O

5 CLASSIFICATION OF VOWELS AND CONSONANTS

Vowels may be defined with an open approximation without any obstruction, partial or complete, in the air passage. They are referred to as vocoids in phonetics. The syllable is a unit of pronunciation consisting of a vowel alone or of a vowel with one or more consonants. A vowel is the nucleus and consonant is a marginal element in the syllable.

Hence a consonant has been defined by most modern phoneticians and linguists as a sound which is produced by a stoppage or partial stoppage of the breath, that is to say, in the production of a consonant the movement of air from the lungs is partially or fully obstructed as a result of narrowing or a complete closure of the air passage, those which can be pronounced independently are vowels: those which need support of others in pronunciation are consonants and (consonants are secondary colors like brown, purple, orange, violet, saffron, green, etc.).

These colors are the product of three primary colors of red, yellow and blue (act like vowels). Similarly consonants are the products of the combinations of different sounds which articulated with the help of vowels.

VOWELS :

𝘻, 𝟏, 𝟏, 𝟏, 𝟕, 𝟓, 𝟔, 𝟗, 𝟐, 𝟑, 𝟓, 𝟔, and 𝟔

(i) **Front vowels :** /𝟏, 𝟕, 𝟗/ While articulation the front of the tongue is raised towards the hard palate. For example, / i,i:,e:,a/ in Hindi, and /i, i:, e, æ/ in English. Hence, /𝟏/, /𝟕, /𝟗/ **are front half-open unrounded vowel.**

(ii) **Back vowels:** /𝟏, 𝟏, 𝟓, 𝟐, 𝟔/ during the production of which the back of the tongue is raised towards the soft palate. Example /o:, u, u:/ in Hindi and /a: u, u:/ in English. Therefore, **back open rounded vowel.** /𝟔/ While articulation, the back of the tongue rise towards uvula, mouth remains opened about inch followed by chin-up slightly and lips are in neutral position. Hence, it is a **back half-open unrounded vowel.**

(iii) **An open vowel:** It is produced with the tongue as low as possible and the jaws are wide open, example /a, a:/ in

English. Hence, /&, &, &, &/ are **back open unrounded vowel.**

(iv) **Central vowels:** It is said when central part of the tongue is raised but here, /ᴑ/is articulated by the back of the tongue is raised towards the soft palate to a height between the half-close and close positions. Lips are rounded, hence it is **centralized back rounded vowel between half-close and close positions.**

CONSONANTS:

&, ℰ, &, &, &, ℴ, \, ⌇, ⅄, &, ⅃, ⅂,

⅏, ⅂, ⅃, ⅄, ⌿, ℱ, ℴ, ℱ, ℿ, ⅃, ⅃, ℰ, ⅄, ⅃, ℰ, ℱ, and ℴ

Classification of Consonants: Consonantal sounds are classified on the basis of the following :

(i)   Voicing,
(ii) Place of articulation,
(iii) Manner of articulation.

Voicing. On the basis of voicing, sound can be classified into voiced and voiceless sounds. The voiced sounds in English are / b,d,g,v,z,m,n,l,r,w,j,ŋ,ð,ʤ,d etc.

(i)   The voiced sounds in Hindi are /ग,घ,ज,झ,ड,द,ढ,घ,ब,भ,य,र,ल,व,म,न/ and the voiced sounds in Wancho are /&,&,&,&,ℱ,ℰ,⌇,\,⅃,ℴ,ℱ,⅏/ other nasalized consonants and all vowels. All the vocoids and semi-vowels are voiced sound, whereas among the consonants some are voiced and some are voiceless. If the vocal cords vibrate when a sound is produced, it is said to be voiceless.

The Place of Articulation. Consonants are divided as given in the following table on the basis of the articulatory points at which the articulators actually touches, or are at their closest.

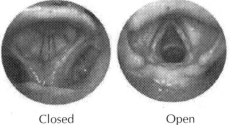

Closed   Open
Figure 4

VOCALCORDS

When this vocal cords are relaxed, they open to let air in and out for breathing. To make sounds, the vocal cords are pulled taut as controlled bursts of air are pushed out from the lungs, to make the closed vocal cords vibrate. The tongue and lips turn these sounds into recognizable speech as shown in figure-4.

.

A table:

(Classification of consonants in respect to Articulations)

Classification	Articulators	Examples of English	Examples of Hindi	Examples of Wancho
Bilabial	Upper lip and lower lip	/p b m w/	प फ ब भ म	/ɛ,ᴑ,ɩ,ɛ/
Dental	Teeth and tip of tongue	/ θ ð /	त थ द ध न	/ɪ,ɛ,ㄥ/
Labio dental	Lower lip and upper teeth	/f v/	व	/⇀,ℱ/
Labio Velar	Back of the togue and soft palate	/w/	ठ	/ᴔ/
Alveolar	Alveolar(teeth) ridge and lip and blade of tongue	/t d s z r l n/	र ल स	/ɛ,ᴦ,ℒ, ℒ,ᴧ,ℵ/
Post alveolar	Hard palate and tip of tongue	/r/	र ट ठ ढ ण	/ℐ, ℑ/
Palato alveolar	Hard palato alveolar and tip, blade and front of tongue	/tʃ/ / ʃ/dʒ/		
Retroflex	Hard palato and tip of tongue curled back	/ʈ/	त ठ ड ढ ण र	/ᴖ/
Palatal	Hard palate tip and front of tongue	/j/	च छ ज झ अ य श ज	/ᴦ,ᴦ;ℰ,ℒ,ℰ/
Velar	Soft palate and back of tongue	/k g n/	क ख ग घ ङ	/ᴨ,ℰ,ᴧ,ℱ/
Glottal Epiglottal or Glottal Stops	Glottis (vocalcords)	/h/ /ʔ ʔ/	ह	/ᴑ,ᴧ/

See Linguistices & Phonetics Edition-2005-06, P: 49, 50, 53.

Identification of Consonants

We can describe and identify a consonant briefly by using a three-term label, indicating (i) whether the sound is voiceless or voiced, (ii) the place of articulation; and (iii) the manner of articulation. For example, /p/ in pant can be described as a voiced, bilabial stop (or plosive), /b/ in bet as a voiced, bilabial stop, /m/ in mango as voiced bilabial nasal, / ŋ/ in hand as a voiced velar nasal, /z/ in zoo as a voiced alveolar fricative, /t ʃ/ in chair as a voiceless palate-alveolar affricate; /f/ in fan as a voiceless labio-dental fricative, and so on so forth. We should have described the consonants of English in these terms while dealing with the phonology of English, but we list them below to facilitate study:

PLOSIVES OR STOPS

A plosive or stop consonant is one that is produced with a stricture. The articulators are in firm contact for some time and then are separated suddenly. These are /p/,/b/,/t/,/d/,/k/, /ℓ/,/ʌ,/ ℰ/, /ᾼ/, /ℰ/, and/g, /Ϭ/. Of this /p/, /ℓ/, /ʌ/ and /b/ are bilabial, /t, ℰ/ and /d, ℰ/ are alveolar, and /k, ᾼ/ and /g, Ϭ/ are velar.

AFFRICATES

An affricate is produced with a complete closure, but the articulators are separated slowly so that some friction is heard. It is to be remembered that friction heard while articulating an affricate is of shorter duration than that heard during the articulation of a fricative. These are affricates, /t ʃ /, /ᾼ/ and /dʒ/ . all are palato-alveolar.

NASALS

A nasal consonant is produced by a complete oral closure. That is, the oral passage of air is completely blocked by the articulators coming into firm contact with each other, but the soft palate is lowered so that the nasal passage of air is open.

The air has thus a free passage through the nose. They are /m, ℰ/ bilabial,/n,ᒐ/alveolarand/ℱ,ŋ/velar.   .

FRICATIVES

A fricative is articulated with a stricture of close approximation: that is, the two articulators are brought so close to each other that the gap between them is very narrow. The air that is compressed by pressured from the lungs escapes through the narrow gap with audible friction. These are /f, →/, and /ℱ, v/ : labiodentals fricatives, / θ / and /ð/ dental fricatives, /ℒ,s/ and / z/ alveolar-fricatives, / ʃ/, / ʒ/and /ℱ / palato-alveolar fricatives and /h/ glottal fricative of these. /f/, /s/, / θ / ʃ/ and /h/ are voiceless and /v/,/ð/,/ʃ,z/and/ʒ/are voiced..

LATERAL

A lateral consonant is articulated with a complete closure in the centre of the vocal tract the air escaping along the sides of the tongue as /l, ⅃/. They are voiced alveolar lateral.   .

FRICTIONLESS CONTINUANT

A frictionless continuant is articulated with an open approximation of the articulators, so that the air passes between the articulators without any friction. Thus the sound is vowel like, but it is included in the list of consonants because it never functions as the nucleus of a syllable. There are frictionless continuant which symbolized by /r, ⅃, ⅃/. These are voiced post-alveolar frictionless continuant.

SEMI-VOWELS

A semi-vowel is a vowel glide to a more prominent sound in the same syllable. Examples of semi-vowels are /j, ʃ/ and /w, ℳ/. Where /j,ʃ/ are a palatal semi-vowel, /w,ℳ/ are a labio-velar semi-vowel.

GLOTTAL STOPS

The sound so produced when completely closing and opening the glottis such as /t, ⟨, /. Examples:- 't' as in butter, '⟨' as in ⟨⟨ (Nah-Bees), ⟨⟨ (Pah-spear), ⟨⟨ (Dah-Nerves), ⟨⟨ (Nuh-Breast), ⟨⟨ (Juh-Mice), ⟨⟨ (Tuh-Spine), etc. in Wancho. Glottal Stop follows the sounds of pre-fix letter(s) , such as - ⟨⟨ (pAh), ⟨⟨ (tEh), ⟨⟨ (pIh), ⟨⟨ (Oh), ⟨⟨ (tUh). Here, 'h' is use as glottal stop compare to- '⟨' or ⟨ ' which follows the sounds of − (A, E, I, O, U),'' it has no sound of its own, it carries flexible sounds.

---

6 SPEECH MECHANISM

The human vocal system can produce a very large number of different speech sounds, Members of a particular speech. Due to such complex mechanism in our vocal cavity each and every parts or place involved in producing varieties of sounds. Exact and appropriate articulation/pronunciation can be spoken only if we can move and place tongue at proper area. Therefore, it is very important to know about the internal and external parts of speech organ system. The following given figure is the human speech organ system.

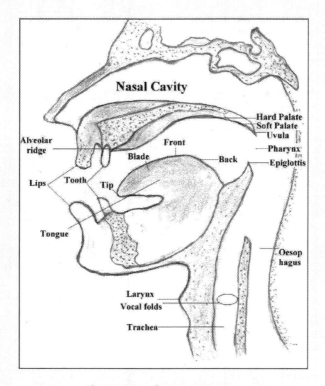

Fig.5 : Speech Organ System

Some of the letters produce unfamiliar and peculiar sounds which cannot be written on the paper using Roman and Hindi/Devnagri script, such type of letters are as ℕ, ꞧ, ꞩ, ꞣ, ꞩ, ꞥ, ꞧ.

The speech organs involve producing a sound by letter ℕ, while speaking are the tip of the tongue touches the alveolar ridge, air passes through both side of tongue, lips and teeth keeps open as shown in figure-6.

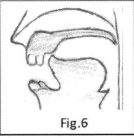

Fig.6

While speaking letter ꞣ, tongue comes downward away from alveolar (Upper roof), a i r passes through both nasal cavity and mouth, lips come closer as shown in figure f-7.

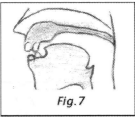

Fig.7

While speaking, ꞩ back of the tongue touches uvula, air passes through both mouth and nasal cavity as shown in figure f-8.

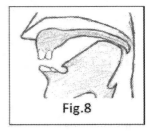

Fig.8

While speaking, ꞥ mouth open wide air passes through both mouth and nose as shown in figure f- 9.

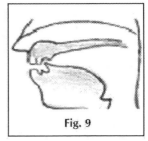

Fig. 9

While speaking, ⊐ corner of the mouth open wide air passes through the narrow gap between the front hard palate and tip of tongue as shown in figure f-11, below:

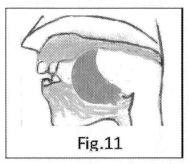

Fig.11

PUNCTUATION

The marks use in writing that divide sentences and phrases are called punctuation. For every languages punctuation is very important without it, words would follow each other in an endless stream and meaning would be lost, the rule of Punctuation is to make the meaning clear.

The Wancho Script also required punctuations to make the sentences meaningful and clear so, punctuation of English will be used in Wancho language (script). Here are a few simple examples:-

Full stop (.), Colon (:), Semicolon (;), Comma (,), Question mark (?), Exclamation mark (!), Inverted comma (" "), Brackets ( ), [], {}, Oblique (/), Dash (-) etc.

ハλ૭

APU

अपू

GRANDFATHER

दादाजी

* llll/lll*

BASA/GASA

बासा／गासा

PINEAPPLE

अनानास

ハハヒ૭/ llhヒ૭

CHAHNU/THAHNU

च:नू/था:नू

TIGER

बाघ

Glottal Stops, IPA symbol "ʔ" is used in English and Colon [:] is used in Hindi

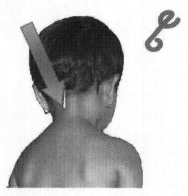

ᰳᰦ/ᰦᰳ
DING/ZING
दिङ/जिङ

NECK
गरदन

ᰃᰦ/ᰦᰃ
GON/JON
गोन/जोन

GOAT
बकरा

ᰃᰪᰦ/ᰦᰃᰪ
NYA/NGA
ञया/ङा

MITHUN (Bos Frontalis)
मिथुन

ꞏ꞉

PHONE
फोन

PHONE
दूरॉभाष

LUK/JUKNGA
लुक/जूकड़ॉं

FROG
मेंदक

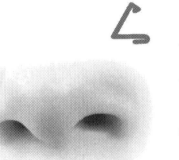

NAKõ
नाकों

NOSE
नाक

ᕕᕊ

PU

पु

SNAKE

साँप

ᕽᛦ / ᑊᛦ

TONG/CHONG

तों/चें

BASKET

टोकरी

ᛦᛦ / ᑎᛦᛦ / ᑊᛦᛦ / ᛉᑎ

THA/ΘLA/CHA/TSHOK

था/थ्ला/चा/चसक

LEG

टांग

FAGONG/BONGPHE/ PHOBONG/GAAM

फगों/बंफे/फांबों/गाम

MAIZE

मक्का

SHAN/HAN

शान/हान

CRAB

केकड़ा

SHAT

शात

WATERFALL

झरना

ᘔᘔ/ᘔᘔ/ᘔᘔ

ZANG/GANG/RANG
जंग/गंग/रंग

SKY
गगन

ᘔᘔ/ᘔᘔ/ᘔᘔ

Zā/Gā/GO
ज़ाँ/गाँ/गो

BONE
हड्डी

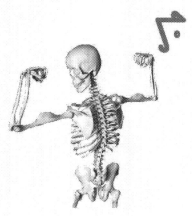

ᘔᘔ/ᘔᘔ

WAK/GAK
वक/गक

PIG
सूअर

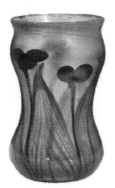

_ﮩﮩ/ﮩﮩ/ﮩﮩ_

VAN/LAIHON/LAIKON

वान/लाइहन/लाइकन

GLASS

काँच

_ﮩﮩ/ﮩﮩ_

KI/HEE

की/ही

DOG

कुत्ता

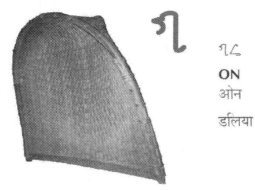

_ﮩﮩ_

ON

ओन

डलिया

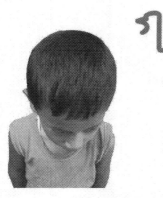

ꯈꯥ/ꯈꯣ/ꯈꯪ
KHAW/KHO/KHANG
खउ/खो/खं

HEAD
सिर

ꯔꯥꯏꯅꯣ
RHINO
राईनो

ꯃꯥꯏꯁ/ꯃꯥꯏꯉꯦꯛ/
ꯃꯥꯏꯅꯛ
MAISA/MAINYEK/
MAINAK
माइसा/माईञोक/माईनक

MONKEY
बंदर

ꓥꓷ

ꆺ꒝/ꆺ꒞ꆺ
KHō/KHUA
खॉं/खोआ

PLATE
तश्तरी

ꇋ

ꆺꇋ
HING
हिङ

MEDICINE
दवा

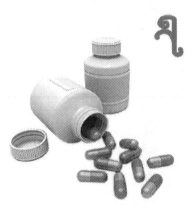

ꆹ

ꆹꇋꉕꆹ/ꆹꇋꆹ ꇋꆹ
LETNU/LENNU
लेलू/लेननू

MOON
चंद्रमा

Z এঢ
LOI
लोई

BUFFALO
भैंस

ৡঙ/ৡঙ
NGO/NGAW
ङो/ङाउ

BANANA
केला

৬মঢ়ঽ/৬মঢ়ঽৠঢ়ৠ
UKHUH/UKHUKNGOPA
उखू:/उखु:ङोंपा

OWL
उल्लू

Glottal Stops, IPA symbol '?' is used in English and Colon [:] is used in Hindi

ᛁᛟ/ᛊᛁ/ᛞᛁ
ᛁθLK/CHAK/SHAK
थ्लक/चक/शक

HAND
हाथ

ᛉᛉᛁ/ᛊᛉᛁ
TSIK/TIK
च्सीक/तिक

POT
बर्तन

ᛉᛉᛙ
TRAʔ
PADDY
धान

Glottal Stops, IPA symbol 'ʔ' is used in English and Colon [:] is used in Hindi

ॐ \ᤕᤕ
LONG
लौं/लोङ

STONE
पत्थर

ᤕ ᤕᤕ/ᤕᤕ/ᤕᤕ
THANG/CHANG/ᤕᤕLANG
थां/चां/थ्लङ

WANCHO SWORD
तलवार

ᤕᤕ/ᤕᤕ
HING/DING
हिं/दिङ

CHILLI
मिर्च

𑌥/𑌥𑌥
SHō/SHUA
सों/सोअ

RIVER
नदी

𑌥/𑌥𑌥
LEYN/LEA
लें

COT
पलंग

𑌥𑌥
OLā
ओलाँ

EAGLE
गरुड़

ॐ ९८७७७ / ८८७
NYAM/BAI
ञाम/बाई

GONG
धंटा

ॐ ९८'ॐ
GINGER
अदरक

ॐ ९८८७
NYAH
ज्या:

FISH
मछली

Following are not in alphabetical order :

८८७
PAH
पा:

SPEAR
शूल

𑜊𑜢𑜑/𑜊𑜢𑜇𑜤𑜑

JUH/JUPHUH

जुः/जुफूः

RAT

चूहा

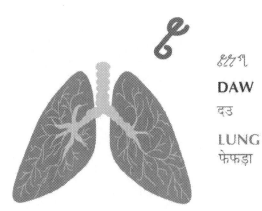

𑜈𑜃

BAN

बन

FIRE

आग

𑜃𑜃𑜈𑜄

DAW

दउ

LUNG

फेफड़ा

ৰ

৬৭৭

GEE
गि

THREAD
धागा

ঙ

৮৮৭

MIA
मया

CAT
बिल्ली

ও

ও৬৭

PHU
फू

UMBRELLA
छाता/छतरी

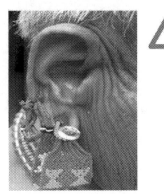

NA

ना

EAR

कान

TON

तोन

HOUSEFLY

मख्खी

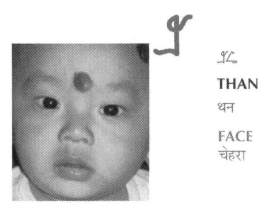

THAN

थन

FACE

चेहरा

ZU

जू

ROPE

रस्सी

KAU

काउ

LADDER

सीढ़ी

ROCKET OR

MISSILE

रौकिट

रॉकिट

ᰃᰕᰜ

MIK

मिक

EYE

आँख

ᰆᰮᰜ

KHOHOM

खहोम

HAT

टोपी

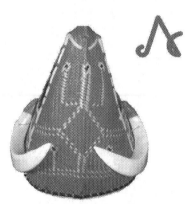

ᰕᰜ

HUM

हम

HOME

घर

ᱤᱨᱚᱯᱞᱮᱱ
एरोप्लेन

AEROPLANE
हवाई जहाज

ᱫᱤ
DI
दी

SHIELD
ढाल

ᱫᱟᱰᱛᱟᱢ
MONGTAM
मोङतम

HEART
दिल

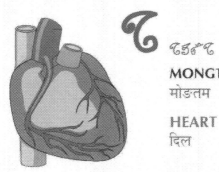

ᝀᝌᝀ
ग्रेप
GRAPE
अंगूर

ᝀᝌᝌ
NYEM
जेम
CROCODILE
मगर

ᝀᝌᝌᝌ
MAIHU
माइहू
COW
गाय

ᝀᝌᝀ
NGUN
डुन
MONEY
रुपये

8 Articulation of Alphabet (Letters) with examples

Wancho Alphabet Symbols & IPA Symbols	Devnagri Symbols	Phonetics symbols, pronunciation/ articulations and some examples in English, Hindi and Wancho

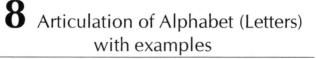 /a/ आ

/ꗇ/ or /a/ During the articulation, the back of the tongue is in the fully open position. It is very low in the mouth; the lips are neutral. Hence, it is a back open unrounded vowel. It is represented by a letter like a, au, in (laugh), e in (clerk) and ea in (heart) respectively. Examples in Wancho language:

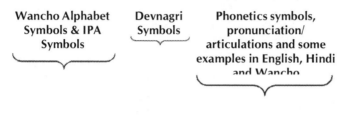

ꗇ𝘩ꗇ(Apaअपा) = Father   ꗇ𝘓ꝏ(Anuअनू) = Mother

ꗇ𝘓ꝏ(Apu अपू) = Grandather   ꗇ𝘓Z(Api अपी) = Grandmother

𝘓 /b/ बू

/𝘓/ Articulation. The two lips make a firm contact with each other. The soft palate is raised, thereby shutting off the nasal passage. Air that is compressed by pressure from the lungs, escapes with an explosive sound when the two lips are separated. Vocal cords vibrate producing voice. Thus it is a voice bilabial plosive. /𝘓/ is represented by /b/, use in words like ball, boy, big and brother. Examples in Wancho:

𝘓ꗇꝏ (bau बाउ) = Satan/Devil   𝘓ꝏ𝘯 (buk बुक) = Book

𝘓𝘯 (bək बक) = Finish   𝘓𝘓 (bən बन) = Fire

ꭢ /t ʃ/   चॖ

/ꭢ/or , during the articulation the tip and blade of the tongue make a firm contact with the teeth ridge. Simultaneously, the front of the tongue is raised in the direction of the hard palate. The palate is raised to shut off the nasal passage of air. Tip of the tongue is separated very slowly from the teeth ridge so that fraction is heard and the sound

produced as voiceless palato-alveolar affricate. /t ʃ/is represented by 'ch' as in cheap, church, cheat, etc. Examples in Wancho.

ꭢ⳼ꭢ(Chah चा:) = Soil   ꭢ⳽⳽(cham चम) = Food
ꭢ⳽⳽(chem चेम) = What?   ꭢꭗ⳾(chik चिक) = pot

ꭤ /d/   द

/ꭤ/ articulated by the tip or blade of the tongue making a firm Contact against the teeth ridge. The soft palate is raised thereby blocking the nasal passage of air. When tip and blade of the tongue is release from the teeth ridge, the air that is compressed by pressure from the lungs escapes with an explosive sound and vibrating vocal cords producing voice as voiced alveolar plosive. It is represented by a letter /d/ in dog, dig and done etc. Examples inWancho.

ꭤ⳼ꞵ(dau दउ) = Lung   ꭤꭗꭢ(ding दिङ) = Neck
ꭤ⳼ꞵ(du दु)   = Deep   ꭤꭗꭗ(dee दि)   = Die

Ꮮ /g/   ग

During the articulation of /Ꮮ/, the back of the tongue makes a firm contact with the soft palate. The soft palate is raised, thereby shutting off the nasal passage of air. The air that is compressed by pressure from the lungs, escapes with an explosive sound when the back of the tongue is released from the soft palate without vibration of vocal cords. Hence, it is voiceless velar plosive. It is represented by the letter /g/ as in get, glory, bag and ago. Examples in Wancho.

Ꮮ⳼ᏞᏞ(Goon गून) = Grave   Ꮮꭗꭢ(Goi गोइ) = Friend
ᏞᏞᏞ(Gan गन्न)   = Shame   Ꮮꭢ(Giगी) = Cane.

ᴸ /j/   यॄ

During the articulation of /ᴸ/ the back of the tongue rose towards the soft palate, slightly, shutting off the nasal passage of air. The front of the tongue assumes a position for a vowel between close and half-close which vibrate vocal cords, producing voice. Hence, it is voiced unrounded palatal semi vowel. If we use /j/ in a word "YOU" it occupied the place of yo as u (you) that is (nang, in Wancho).

Example-

Depart = ᶜᴸⁱᴸ(Nyan ज्ञान)	Mithun = ᶜᴸⁱ(Nya ज्ञ)
Fish = ᶜᴸⁱ𝒫(Nyiaʔ ज्ञाः)	Yellow = ᶜᴸⁱⁱᴸ(Nyaan ज्ञान)

etc.

⊙ /ph/   फ़ॄ

During the articulation of /⊙/, the lips make a firm contact with each other. The air that is compressed by the pressure from the lungs, escapes with an explosive sound when lips open. The vocal cords are held apart without vibration; hence it is voiceless bilabial plosive. /⊙/ is represented by letter /ph/ as in phone, physical, phylum, physics, etc. Example in Wancho.

⊙ᴸᴸ(phon फोन) = Burst	⊙ℓᴢ(phai फाई) = Late
⊙⑨(phing फीं) = swell	⊙ᴸ(phang फाँ) = Down/under/below

\ /l/   ल्ॄ

/ \ / articulated by the tip of the tongue making a firm contact against the teeth ridge. There is thus a complete closure in the middle of the mouth. The soft palate is raised so as to shut off the nasal passage of the air completely. The side of the tongue is lower so that the lung air is free to escape along side of the tongue without any friction. Vocal cords vibrate to produced voice thus, it is voiced alveolar lateral. /\/ represented by the letter /L/ as in leave, life, love, long etc. Example in Wancho.

\ᴸ(lam लम) = Road	\ᴸᴸ⑨(Longding लोंदिङ) = Longding
\⑨(Ling लिं) = Forest	\ᴸᴸᴸᴸ (Lennu लेन्नु) = Moon

Glottal Stops, IPA symbol 'ʔ' is used in English and Colon [:] is used in Hindi

∠ /n/   नॄ

/∠/ during the articulation, the tip of the tongue makes a firm Contact with the teeth ridge, thus blocking off the oral passage of air completely. The soft palate is lower so that the air escapes through the nose. The vocal cords vibrate producing voice thus it is voiced alveolar nasal. /∠/ is represented by letter /n/ as in name, near, nice, neck and noun etc. Examples in Wancho.

∠𝟞(Nang नां) = You   ∠Z(Ni नी) = Laugh
∠ℒ(Na ना) = Ear   ∠ℒ⁀(Nah नाः / नअः) = Bee

𝒜 /p/   पॄ

/𝒜/ during the articulation the two lips make a firm contact with each other. The soft palate is raised, thereby shutting off the nasal passage. Air that is compressed by pressure from the lungs, escapes with an explosive sound when the two lips are separated. Vocal cords held apart without vibration. Thus it is a voiceless bilabial plosive. /𝒜/ is represented by /p/, use in words like pill, pussy, pig and prayer. Examples in wancho.

𝒜∠(pan पन) = Tree   𝒜𝟞𝟞 (Pu पू / पउ) = Snake
𝒜ℒℒZ(Paai पाई) = Cotton   𝒜𝟞ℒ𝟞(Patau पताउ) = Pongchau

𝔒 /t/   तॄ

/𝔒/ is articulated by the tip and blade of the tongue making a firm contact against the teeth ridge. The soft palate is raised thereby blocking the nasal passage of air. When the tip or blade of the tongue is released from the teeth ridge, the air that is compressed by pressure from the lungs escapes with an explosive sound. The vocal cords do not vibrate hence, voiceless alveolar plosive. It is represented by /t/ in english letter, use as in tea, torch, teacher, time, at, stain, etc. Example in Wancho.

𝔒𝟞𝟞(Tume तूम) = Salt   𝔒Zℿ (Tik तिक) = Pot
𝔒ℒ(Ta ता) = 20(Twenty)   𝔒ℐ⁀(Teh तेः / तए:) = Cut

Glottal Stops, IPA symbol 'ʔ' is used in English and Colon [:] is used in Hindi

ʃ /θ/   थ़

/ʃ/ while articulation, the tip of the tongue makes a light contact with the edge of the upper front teeth. The soft palate is raised so as to shut off the nasal passage of air. The air escapes through the narrow space between the tip of the tongue and the front teeth, causing audible friction. The vocal cords do not vibrate, it articulates similar or Exactly /θ/ in english. Thus it is a voiceless dental fricative. /ʃ/ is Represented by letters th as in thin, thick, path etc. Example in wancho.

ʃ乚(Thn/Than थन) = Face   ʃ乚乚 (Thun थून) = Lime

ʃ乚乙乙(Thai थई) = Storm   ʃ乙乙(Thee थि) = Intestine

→ /f/   फ़

/→/during the articulation the lower lip is brought very close to the Upper front teeth so that the gap between them is extremely narrow. The soft palate is raised and thus the nasal passage of air is blocked completely. The air escapes through the narrow gap between the lower lip and the upper front teeth with audible friction. Vocal cords held wide apart without vibration, it is thus voiceless labio-dental fricative, as represented by /f/ as in five, food, fill, fine etc. Example in Wancho.

→Ə(Fing फ़ी) = Swell   →乙乙(Fai फ़ई) = Late/behind

(This sound generally found in Wakka circle especially in upper region of Wancho.)

ℒ /s/   स़

/ℒ/ is articulated by placing the tip and blade of the tongue very near the Teeth ridge so that the space between them is very narrow. The soft palate is raised, shutting off the nasal passage of air. The vocal cords do not vibrate. Air escapes through the narrow gap between the tip and blade of the tongue and Teeth ridge with audible friction. Thus, it is voiceless alveolar fricative (sibilant). And it is represented by letter /s/ in English as in sin, same, son and singing etc. Example in Wancho.

ℒ乙乙(soi सोई) = vegetable   ℒ乆ℱ(sung सूङ) = umbilical

ℒ乙ℒ(shan सान) = Crab   ℒ乙ℰ(som सोम) = Prayer

𝒮 / ʃ/,sh　　　　श्

/𝒮/ while articulation the tip of the tongue raised very near the Teeth ridge so that the space between them is very narrow. The soft palate is also raised, shutting off the nasal passage of air. Mouth open slightly wide. The vocal cords do not vibrate. Air escapes through the narrow gap between the tip and blade of the tongue and Teeth ridge with audible friction. Thus, it is voiceless alveolar fricative (sibilant). And it is represented by letter /sh/ in English as in shine, shell, ship and shelter etc. Example in Wancho.

𝒮𝓁𝓉ℰ (shat शात) = Waterfall　　　𝒮𝓁𝓉𝓁𝓛 (shaan शान) = Wet
𝒮𝓩𝓛𝓛ᴙ (shinnu शिन्नु) = Stomach
(Symbol Dot (.) will be pronounced as tup while dictate)

ᴦ /dʒ/　　　　ज्

/ᴦ/ while articulation the tip and blade of the tongue comes very near the teeth ridge so that the space between them is very narrow. The soft palate is raised, shutting off the nasal passage of air. The vocal cords vibrate producing voice. The air escapes through the narrow gap between the tip and blade of the tongue and teeth ridge with audible friction. Thus it is voiced palate-alveolar fricative (sibilant). /ᴦ/ is pronounce similar to letter /j/ in English as in Jesus, January, Jeep and Jeans etc. Example in Wancho.

ᴦᴕᴩ(juh/juh जू:) = Rat　　　　　ᴦᴙ𝓛(jon जोन) = Goat
ᴦᴢᴨ(jik जिक) = Necklace　　　　ᴦᴕ(ju जु) = Wine/alcohol

ᴦ̇ /z/　　　　ज्

/ᴦ̇/ is articulated exactly or very near to /z/ the tip and blade of the tongue comes very near the teeth ridge so that the space between them is very narrow. The soft palate is raised, shutting off the nasal passage of air. The vocal cords vibrate producing voice with audible friction. Thus it is voiced alveolar fricative (sibilant). /ᴦ̇/ is pronounce similar to letter /z/ in English as in zoo, zero and zee etc. Example in Wancho.

ᴦ̇ᴕ (zu जु) = Rope　　　　　ᴦ̇𝓁𝓛 (zan जान) = Iron
ᴦ̇ᴙ (zo * जों) = Bamboo　　　ᴦ̇ᴕᴨ (zuk जूक) = Graveyard
(Symbol Dot (.) will be pronounced as tup while dictate)

ᘱ /w/ व्

/ᘱ/ during articulation the soft palate is raised to shut off the nasal passage And blocked air completely. The back of the tongue is raised in the direction of the soft palate to the position for a vowel between-close and half- close and the lips are rounded, then the tongue quickly glides to the position of the flowing vowel. The position of the lips also changes depending upon the immediately following vowel. The vocal cords vibrate, producing voice, thus it is a voiced rounded labio-velar semi-vowel. It is represented by a letter /w/ in English as in wife, wish, wise, waste, woman and want etc. Example In Wancho.

ᘱ𝓏𝓛ᐃ (Wanu वानू) = Wanu village

ᘱ𝓛𝓒𝓢 (wanmang वनमं) = Dream

𝓟 /v/ व्

/𝓟/ is articulated by the lower lip is brought very close to the upper front teeth So that the gap between them is extremely narrow. The soft palate is raised and thus the air of the nasal passage is blocked completely. The air escapes through the narrow gap between the lower lip and the upper front teeth with audible friction. The vocal cords vibrate producing voice, thus it is a voiced labio-dental fricative. It is represented by a letter /v/ as in veil, van, voice, view etc. Example in wancho.

𝓟𝓏ᐃ(vaw/vau वाउ) = Satan/Devil   𝓟𝓛(Van वन) = Fire

𝓟𝓛𝓀𝓏(Vanpa बनपा) = Guest

ᘁ /k/ क्

/ᘁ/ during the articulation the back of the tongue makes a firm contact with the soft palate. The soft palate is raised, thereby shutting off the nasal cavity of air. The air that is compressed by pressure from the lungs escapes with an explosive sound when the back of the tongue is released from the soft palate. The vocal cords do not vibrate, thus it is described as a voiceless velar plosive. It is represented by a letter /k/ in English, क in devnagri as in king, kind, kill etc. Example in Wancho.

ᘁᘛ𝓏 (Koi कोइ) = me   ᘁᘛ𝓛𝓛ᐃ (Konnu कोन्नू) = Konnu village

ᘁ𝓙𝓒 (kem केम) = We   ᘁᐃ (ku कू) = Me

ᘁ𝓒 (kam कम) = Home

ɔ:/   ओ/ो

/ꞏ/ during the articulation, the back of the tongue is in the fully open position. The lips are rounded while pronouncing the letter. Hence it is a back open rounded vowel. In English symbol it is represented by /ɔ:/ which is similar but not exact with the articulation of /ꞏ/. It is represented by letter /o/ in English as in onion, owl, ozone, omnipresent etc. Examples in Wancho language.

ꞏ𝓛ꞇ (ova ओवा) = Who   ꞏ𝓛ꞇꞈ (opak ओपाक) = Duck
ꞏ𝓛9 (oshing ओसीं) = Selfish

ꞏ /aʊ/   अउ

/ꞏ/ at the time of articulation, back of the tongue is raised towards the soft palate as /oꞏ/ in Hindi, /ɔ:/ in English as in caught, laugh, taught etc. Therefore, it is back open rounded vowel. Examples in Wancho language.

ꞏꞷ (ou/"u or aʊ/" अउ)= (Meaning MOTHER in Mintong village and HEN in Khasa village)
ⴟꞏ (Khau खउ)= Head   ꞏꞏ(Hau हउ)= Cage

ꓩ /r/   र

/ꓩ/ is articulated by the tip of the tongue is raised in the direction of the hinder part of the teeth ridge. The soft palate is raised to shut off the nasal passage of the air. The air from the lungs comes out through the gap between the tip of the tongue and the post-alveolar region without any friction. The vocal cords vibrate to produce voice hence; it is a voiced post-alveolar frictionless continuant (alveolar trill), represented by /r/ in English as in Rome, read, run, right etc. Example in Wancho.

ꓩ6(Rang रां) = God   ꓩꞷ𝓛ꞇ(Rusa रूसा) = Rusa village
ꓩ9(Ring रीं) = Sky

(र, R or ꓩ are mostly use by the people staying in lower region of Wancho like Kannuwari, Rusa,Runnu etc. In upper region it is almost absent.)

௶ /m/ म्

௶/ articulation, the two lips are brought together and thus the oral passage Of air is blocked completely. Soft palate is lowered and air escapes through the nose. The vocal cords vibrate followed by producing voice, thus it is voiced bilabial nasal. /௶/ is represented by /m/ in english letter as in mother, money, mouse, Mary etc. Example in Wancho.

௶௷ (Māng मं) = Dead body   ௶ℓℤℤ (Maie मई) = Meat
௶ℤՈ (Mik मिक) = Eye   ௶ℓℓ (Ma मा) = Wound
௶ℓℓՈ (Maak माक) = Spider

ᐱ /kh/ ख्

/ᐱ/ at the time of articulation the back of the tongue raised towards the soft palate very closed but do not come to contact, which creates sound of friction due to compressed air pressure coming from the lungs. The vocal cords vibrate thus it is described as a voiceless velar fricative. Represented by /Kh/ as in Khonsa, Khan, Khaki etc. Example in Wancho.

ᐱ৬ℒ (Khun खून) = Poison   ᐱℙℒ (Khon खोन) = Skin
ᐱℙℓ (Kho खो) = Spade   ᐱℓℓℓ6 (Khaat खात) = Gun power
ᐱℓℓᐱ6 (Khaw खाउ) = Wide

९ /h/ ह्

/९/ while articulation the vocal cords are kept close together so that the glottis is very narrow. The air escapes through the narrow glottis with audible friction hence; it is described as a voiceless Epiglottal fricative. It is represented by a letter /h/ in English as in happy, home, holly, hill etc. Example in Wancho.

९௶ (Ham हम) = Home   ९9 (Hing हिङ) = Chilli
९ℤℤ (Hee ही) = Dog   ९6௶ (Hume हुम) = Salt

Glottal Stops, IPA symbol 'ʔ' is used in English and Colon [:] is used in Hindi

⟨ /e/ ए

/⟨/ during the articulation the front of the tongue raised towards the hard palate to a height between the half-open and half-open positions. The lips are neutral. Thus it is a front unrounded vowel between half-open and open positions. It is represented by /æ/ or /e/ in English letter as in aero plane, aim, apple, ass etc. Example in Hindi and Wancho.

⟨Ω (ek/ एक) = One   ⟨⟨(Le/Læ ले) = Tongue
⟨⟨ (at एत) = 8(eight)   ⟨⟨(Tse) = Intestine

Z /i or I/ ई

/Z/ is articulated by the front of the tongue is raised in the direction between the closed and half-close positions, the lips are loosely spread. Thus it is front unrounded vowel between close and half-close positions. Z is represented by /i/ in English letter as in ink, imagine, immediate, illness etc. Example in Wancho.

⟨ZΩ⟨⟨ (Mikse मिकसे) = Tear   ⟨ZΩ (Chik चिक) = Pot
⟨ZΩ (Lik लिक) = Necklace   ⟨ZΩ (Tik तिक) = Sting
⟨ZΩ(Sik सिक) = Pinch

⟨ /ŋ/ŋg/ ङ्

/⟨/ is articulated by the front of the tongue is raised to contact with hard palate, initially air escapes through nose and finally escapes through the mouth cavity. The vocal cords vibrate and produce voice. Hence, it is voiced velar, it is pronounced somewhat like 'Ng' in English as in Ngoma (Tradition drum of southern or eastern Africa). Example in Wancho.

⟨⟨ (Ngo ङो) = Banana   ⟨⟨⟨ (Ngun ङून) = Money
⟨⟨⟨ (Ngaw ङाउ) = Language

Glottal Stops, IPA symbol 'ʔ' is used in English and Colon [:] is used in Hindi

ᘣ /u/ ᴈ

/ᘣ/ during the articulation, the fore part of the back of the tongue is raised towards the soft palate to a height between the half-close and close positions. Lips are rounded, hence it is centralized back rounded vowel between half-close and close positions. It is represented by letter oo, u as in look, loo, book, lull, pull, tune etc. Example In Wancho.

ᘣᴴ (Lung लूङ) = String   ᴧᘣ (Anu अनू) = Mother
ᴧᘣ (Khu खू) = Cloth   ᴖᘣ (Ku कू) = Me

The twelve letters in the next pages produce unique and peculiar sound(s) which are not familiar with English and Hindi Alphabet, even some of them are not recognized in International Phonetics Alphabet (IPA) chart; hence, it is very difficult to compare with the others alphabet while writing. But it is very useful and popular in Wancho Language, due to absence of these letters (sounds) the other script could not hold (write) our language exactly with proper pronunciation.

𝒥𝒰   /ɭ̊/

/𝒰/ is articulate by the blade and tip of the tongue making a firm contact against the hard palate. The soft palate is raised so as to shut off the nasal passage of the air completely. The sides of the tongue remains gap so that the air coming from the lung be freed to escape through the sides of the tongue without any friction. Vocal cords did not vibrate to produce voice thus, it is vioceless retroflex lateral fricative. It is slightly similar to the sound produce by an IPA symbols /ɭ̊/. Mostly these type of sounds are found at the border area of Myanmer such as the villages of Khasa, Khanu, Votnu and Jagan etc. Example in wancho.

𝒥𝒰Ω (ɭ̊lak/thlak)=Hand
𝒥𝒰𝑙𝑧 (ɭ̊la/thla)=Leg
𝒥𝒰6 (ɭ̊lng/thlang/thlng)= Daw/sword

This kind of sound is mostly spoken by the villagers of Khasa, Votnu, Jagan, Khanu while naming hand, leg and daw etc. (Exact pronounciation of sound is available in CD-disc given along with this book).

WIKIPADIA:

The voiceless retroflex lateral fricative is a type of consonantal sound, use in some spoken languages. The IPA has no officially recognised symbol for this sound. However, in the literature the "belt" on the recognized symbol for a voiceless lateral fricative is combined with the tail of the retroflex consonants to create the adhoc symbol [ɭ̊].

Now that font –editing software has become accessible, well-designed graphs for this and other non-sanctioned lateral fricatives will occasionally be seen. In deed, SIL interantional added these symbols to the private use area of their charis and Doulos fonts, with the retroflex as U +F266. In 2008 the unicode Technical committee accepted this character as U +A78E Latin small latter 'L' with retroflex Hook and Belt ', etc.

ᴿ /ts/   च्य्

/ᴿ/ during the articulation the tip of the tongue make a firm contact with the Alveolar ridge. The soft palate is raised to shut off the nasal passage of air. The tip of the tongue is separated very slowly with a slight friction from the teeth ridge so that some friction is heard and the sound produced is voiceless alveolar affricative. ᴿ is represented by /ts/ as in Tsai, Tsailo, Tsak, Tsangtsa, Tsonu etc. Example in Wancho.

ᴿᴸᴸᵉ (Tsai) = Song,   ᴿᴸᴸᶻᴎ (Tsailo) = Distance,
ᴿᴸᴸᶰ (Tsak) = Strong   ᴿᴼᴿᴸᴸ (Tsangtsa) = Body,
                                     ᴿᴸᴸᵇ (Tsonu) = Summer

ꟻ   त्र्

/ꟻ/ while articulation, the tongue is curled back and tip of tongue is raised toward front side of hard palate touching slightly for very short period, corner of the mouth open wide. The air from the lungs escapes through both sides of the tongue with audible friction. Thus, it is voiceless alveolar fricative (sibilant). And it is represented by letter /ꟻ/ Example in Wancho may not be exact.

ᶜᴵᴸᵉ (Trah र्:) = Paddy   ᶜᴼᴸᶜᴵᴸᵉ (तिङखत्र्) = Tingkhatra
ᶜᴵᴸᶰ (Trak र्क) = Strong   ᶜᴵᴸᶜᶻ (Trahchi र्:ची) = Right side

Ʂ /ong /oŋ /   ओं

/Ʂ/ is articulated by the back of the tongue is in the fully open position at the beginning followed by raising of the back of the tongue towards the soft palate which completely shut off the mouth cavity and open the nasal cavity to escape the air coming from lungs and lips are in rounded. Hence, it is back closed rounded vowel. Ʂ is pronounce somewhat like" ong" as in t**ong**ue, l**ong**, s**ong**, wr**ong** etc. Example in Wancho.

ᴧᴿꟅ (Khong खङ) = Run   ᴧᴿꟅꟅ (Khongn खों) = Invitation
ᴠꟅᶿꟿ (Longding लोंडिङ) = Longding Town
ᴠꟅꟅ (Long लों) = Stone   ꟳꟅ (Song सों) = Caterpillar
ᴒꟅꟅ (Kong कों) = Cool)

     (Symbol Dot (.) will be pronounced as tup while dictate)

Ϭ / ʌ ɳ/   अं/अङ

/Ϭ/ while articulation the back of the tongue is fully open position at the beginning followed by raising of the back of the tongue at the direction of soft palate and shutting off the mouth cavity releasing sound ang/aŋ or /Ϭ/ as in f**ang**, **Ang**lo, **ang**rez, **ang**ry, etc. Example in Wancho.

ᒷϬ (zang जं / Rang रं/Gang गं) = Sky
ℱϬ (Chang चां) = Daw/sword
ᴧϬ (Khang खं) = Fore-head
ᴢϬ (Nang नां) = You
ᴓϬ (Wang वां) = Wangham clan
ᴒϬ (Kang कं) = Crack
ᴼϬ (Mang मां) = Deadbody

Ɔ /iɳ /ing/   ईङ

/Ɔ/ during the articulation the front part of the tongue is raised towards the direction of the hard palate followed by the raising of the back of the tongue towards soft palate and uvula, completely shut off the mouth cavity and allow the air coming from the lung to escape through nasal cavity. The sound so produce is somewhat like"ing/iɳ" as in th**ing**, k**ing**, com**ing**, play**ing**, lov**ing**, s**inging** etc. Example in Wancho.

ᴓƆ (phing फिङ) = Swell
ᴺƆ (Hing हिंङ)   = Medicine
ᶠƆ (Ting तिङ)   = village

ᴙ   अँ

/ᴙ/ is articulated by the back of the tongue in fully open position at the beginning than back of the tongue is raised very close to uvula/soft palate, the air escapes partially from both nose and mouth. Lips are rounded; hence it is back-half open rounded vowel. Example in Wancho.

ᴼᴙ (Mõ मों)= Soul   ᴧᴙ (Khõ खों)= Plate

ᴺᴙ (Lõ लों)= Love   ᴝᴙ (Shõ सों)= River

ૐ

/ૐ/ is articulated by front of the tongue raised towards the hard palate followed by the raising of back of the tongue in direction of uvula/soft palate finally blocked the mouth cavity, air escapes through nose only as म न ङ etc. in Hindi. Example in Wancho.

\ૐ (Le* लें) = Cot,   ૮ૐ (Be* बें)= Thigh
૮ૐ (Ne* नें) = Net   \ꝋૐ (Longphe* लंफें) = Soya bean
૬ૐ (Te* तें) = Ginger

ૐ   आँ

/ૐ/ articulation, in the beginning the back of the tongue is fully open position than back of the tongue is raised towards uvula/soft palate to shut off the mouth cavity completely. The lips are spread in normal open position, as – माँ (Mother), हाँ (Yes), etc. in Hindi. Example in Wancho.

ૐૐ (Shā साँ) = Fishing net
ૐૐ (Jā जाँ) = Water (poetic language)
ૐૐ (Kā काँ) = Millet
ૐૐૐ (Jā: जाँ:) = Bone

ૐ /Nyo/   ज़्

/ૐ/ during the articulation the blade of the tongue is raised in the direction of hard palate and touches with slight friction. The air coming from lungs escapes through both nasal and mouth cavity. Lips remain in open normal position hence, it is palatal. Example in Wancho.

ૐૐૐ (Nyam ज्ञम) = Gong   ૐૐૐ (Nyiah ज्ञा:) = Fish
ૐૐૐ (Nyai/Nyae ज्ञाई) = Ice

Glottal Stops, IPA symbol 'ʔ' is used in English and Colon [:] is used in Hindi

ᰧ᱖ U:(Nasal)

/ᰧ᱖/ While articulation, the back of the tongue rose towards uvula, mouth remains opened about inch followed by chin-up slightly and lips are in neutral position. Hence, it is a back half-open unrounded vowel. It cannot be compared with English and Hindi. Examples in Wancho language:

ᰝ᱖ (Pa*) = Listen   ᰕᰝᱺᰩ᱖(kapha*) = Slop
ᰧᰩᱺ᱖ (Khopha*) = pocket   ᰟ᱖(kha*) = Abdomen

(Symbol Dot (.) will be pronounced as tup while dicate)

ᰮ /ʔ‍or ʔ/Yiʔ/yih/   यी:

/ᰮ/ is a glottal stop. It is articulated by epiglottis is raised towards the back wall (Towards back bone) of the pharynx; vocal cords are completely closed and stopped the air travelling in the glottis. It is pronounced somewhat like "Yih" and perform functions similar to 'ʔ' and 't' in English letter as in though, cut, drought, put etc. Example in Wancho.

ᰛᰝᰮ (Naʔ ना:) = Bee   ᰝᰝᰮ (Pah पा:) = Spear
ᰧᰝᰮ (Khaʔ खा:) = Liver   ᰤᰝᰮ (Dah डा:) = Nerves

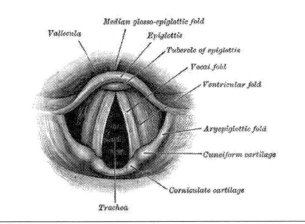

REFERENCE: SEE LINGUISTICS & PHONETICS EDITION: 2005-06, P: 83- 101
Glottal Stops, IPA symbol 'ʔ' is used in English and Colon [:] is used in Hindi

9 SYNONYMS
(Same meaning)

English	Hindi	Wancho	Wancho using Roman/Hindi
Air	वायु	ꗼꙂꝪ꜔Ꝫ, ꗼꙂꝪ꜕Ꝫ, ꝪꝪꝪ꜕Ꝫ	Jangvun जंवून, jangvin जंविन, gangbin गंबिन
Bear	भालु	ꝲꝪꝲꝪ, ꝲꝪꝲꝪ	Chapnu चपनू, thapnu थपनू
Bridge	पुल	ꝪꝪꝪ, ꝪꝪꝪ	Shai साई, hai हाई
Beautiful	सुन्दर	ꝪꝪꝪꝪ, ꝲꝪꝪꝪ, ꝪꝪꝪꝪ	Thamai थामई, chamai चामई, sanmai सनमई
Bone	हडडी	ꝪꝪ, ꝪꝪ	Ga*गाँ, ja* जाँ
Brother	भाई	ꝪꝪꝪꝪ, ꝪꝪꝪꝪ	Achai अचई, atai अतई
Chilli	मिर्च	ꝪꝪ, ꝪꝪ	Hing हिङ, ding दिङ
Clothes	कपड़े	ꝪꝪꝪ, ꝪꝪ, ꝪꝪ	Nee नि, khat खत, khu खू
Cough	खाँसना	ꝪꝪꝪ, ꝪꝪꝪ	Hai हाई, kai काई
Cow	गाई	ꝪꝪꝪꝪꝪ, ꝪꝪꝪꝪ	Maidu माईडु, maihu माईहू
Crab	केकड़ा	ꝪꝪꝪ, ꝪꝪꝪ	Shan सान, han हान
Dog	कुत्ता	ꝪꝪꝪ, ꝪꝪꝪ	Hi ही, ki की
Dream	सपना	ꝪꝪꝪꝪ, ꝪꝪꝪ, ꝪꝪꝪ	Wanmang वनमां, ganmang गनमां, banmang बनमां

---

* symbol shows incomplete pronunciation
Glottal Stops, IPA symbol 'ʔ' is used in English and Colon [:] is used in Hindi

English	Hindi	Wancho	Wancho using Roman/Hindi
Enemy	दुश्मन	*6ttL, SttL*	Gaan गान, jaan जान
Face	चेहरा	*IL* *LL*	Than (than) थन, shan (shn) सन
Fire	आग	*LL, 6L*	Ban बन, gan गन
Fish	मछली	*ELttP*	Nyiah जयाः
Food	भोजन	*6%%, L6* *LttP*	Tam तम्म, shat सत, shah साः
Foot	पैर	*Itt, Ptt* *NItt*	Tha था, cha चा, thla*
Friend	मित्र	*61Z, JtZNtZ* *\6t1Z*	Goi गोइ, roikhoi रोईखोई, lamgoi लमगोई
Frog	मेंढक	*Γ\6Π, \6Π*	Juk जूक, luk लूक
Glass	काँच	*IttL, Γ1PΠtL* *Γ1PLL*	Van वान, johkon जोःकोन, johhon जोःहन
Goat	बकरी	*Γ1L, 61L* *Γ1L*	Jon जोन, gon गोन, zon जोन,
Gong	धंटा	*ELtt%, LttZ* *LLt%*	Nyam जयाम, bai बइ, nam नाम
Grave	कब्र	*6\6L, Γ\6L* *Γ\6Π*	Goon गून, jun जून, zuk जूक
Hand	हाथ	*IΠ, PΠ, NIΠ* *ΓΠ*	Thak , chak, thlak*, jak
Home	धर	*Π%, 1%*	Kam कम, ham हम
Housefly	मख्खी	*116, 61L*	Hot होत, ton तोन
Idea	भाव	*11L, Γ1*	Hon हन, je जए
Intestine	अंतड़ी	*I1, %1, IZZ*	Thea थए, tsea, thi थई

---

* symbol shows incomplete pronunciation
Glottal Stops, IPA symbol '**ʔ**' is used in English and Colon [:] is used in Hindi

English	Hindi	Wancho	Wancho using Roman/Hindi
King	राजा	ᵐᵃ, ᵐᵃ	Wangngm वाँङम, Wangham वाँहम
Lime	चूना		Thun थून, shun सून
Maize	मक्का		Gam गाम, bongphe बोंफे fagong फगों
Mosquito	मच्छर		Munkho मूनखों, haja* हँजँ, hiha हिहा
Mother	माता		Anu अनू, Aju अजू, Anyu अञयू, Au अउ, Amoh अमोः
Mountain	पर्वत		Lingnu लिंनू, kungnu कोंनू
Mouth	मुँह		Chun चुन, tun तून, chap चप
Necklace	कंठहार		Lik लिक, jik जिक
One	एक		Acha अचा, ata अता
Pig	सूअर		Vak बक, gak गक wak वक
Pot	बर्तन		Chik चिक, tik तिक
Room	कमरा		Noi नोई, Nyoi ञोई
Salt	नमक		Tume तूम, hume हूम
Sister	बहन		Aja अजा, ana अना
Sky	गगन		Rang रां, gang गां, jang जां
Soil	मिट्टी		Hah हाः, kah काः, chah चाः
Song	गीत		Tai ताई, tsai
Stag			Thok थोक, tok तोक, chok चोक

* symbol shows incomplete pronunciation
Glottal Stops, IPA symbol 'ʔ' is used in English and Colon [:] is used in Hindi

English	Hindi	Wancho	Wancho using Roman/Hindi
String	रस्सी	ᨠ, ᨠ	Lung लूड., jung जूड.
Sword	तलवार	ᨂ, ᨂ ᨂ	Thang थां, chang चां, thlang
Teacher	शिक्षक	ᨃᨃᨃ	Lainopa लाइनोपा
Tiger	बाघ	ᨃᨃ ᨃᨃ	Chahnu चाःनू thahnu थाःनू
Time	समय	ᨃᨃ	Hanpak हानपक
Torch	टार्च	ᨃᨃ	Phetban फेटबन
Univers	अंतरिक्ष	ᨃᨃ	Gangphangnu गंफंगनू
Watch	घड़ी	ᨃᨃ	Chuthan चूथन
Water	जल	ᨃ	Te ती, chi ची
Wine	शराब	ᨃ	Joo जू
World	संसार	ᨃᨃᨃ ᨃᨃᨃ ᨃᨃᨃ	Chahvannu चाःवान्नू, hahvannu हाःवान्नू , kahvannu काःवान्नू

10 ANTONYMS
(Opposite)

Wancho	Pronounce	English	Wancho	Pronounce	English
𖩑𖩅𖩑	Apa	Father	𖩑𖩌𖩆	Anu	Mother
𖩑𖩌𖩑𖩉	Atai	Brother	𖩑𖩅𖩑	Ana	Sister
𖩑𖩘𖩓	Aho	Uncle	𖩑𖩅𖩉	Ani	Aunty
𖩑𖩅𖩉	Api	Grand Mother	𖩑𖩅𖩆	Apu	Grand Father
𖩊𖩅	Ban	Fire	𖩎𖩉	Chi	Water
𖩉𖩓𖩎𖩑𖩉	Jangngai	Day	𖩉𖩓𖩅𖩓	Jangnak	Night
𖩍𖩚𖩎𖩅𖩓	Latnu	Moon	𖩉𖩓𖩑𖩅𖩅	Janghan	Sun
𖩕𖩉𖩌𖩅𖩓	Mihnu	Female	𖩕𖩉𖩌𖩅𖩑	Mihpa	Male
𖩘𖩓𖩌𖩅𖩕	Hokham	Hot	𖩘𖩓𖩅	Hokong	Cold
𖩘𖩎𖩅	Hojen	New	𖩘𖩎𖩅	Hojang	Old
𖩘𖩑𖩎	Hah	Earth	𖩉𖩅	Jang	Sky
𖩘𖩓𖩕𖩎	Homa*	Bad	𖩘𖩓𖩕𖩑𖩉	Homai	Good
𖩋𖩓𖩓	Sheko*	Girl	𖩍𖩓𖩎	Laka*	Boy
𖩎𖩉𖩅𖩓	Chonu	Summer	𖩊𖩎𖩅𖩓	Banu*	winter
𖩍𖩑𖩎𖩆	Lobang*	Rich	𖩑𖩑𖩉𖩉𖩉𖩑	Taishih	Poor
𖩇𖩑𖩅𖩓	Konu*	Mountain	𖩋𖩑𖩅𖩓	Shonu*	River
𖩑𖩑𖩇𖩅	Taika*	Old man	𖩅𖩑𖩓𖩊𖩑	Nausa	Children

11 SIMILARITIES

(Similar in sound, different in meaning)

(Short Vowel Sounds)			(Long Vowel Sounds)		
Wancho	**English**	**=**	**Wancho**	**English**	
ℓℓ Ba	Gap	=	*ℓℓℓ* Baa	Teeth/Axe	
ℓℓ Ban	Fire	=	*ℓℓℓ* Bann	10(Ten)	
ℓℓ Bea	Group	=	*ℓℓℓ* Bea*	Pull	
ℓℓ Bu	Hot(Chilli)	=	*ℓℓℓ* Boo	Itching/Scabies	
ℓℓ Bo*	Scrotum	=	*ℓℓℓ* Bo*	Song	
ℓℓ Cha	One	=	*ℓℓℓ* Chaa	Remainder	
ℓℓ Cho	Chest	=	*ℓℓℓ* Cho	Summer	
ℓℓ Cham	What	=	*ℓℓℓ* Cham	Food	
ℓℓ Chi	Water	=	*ℓℓℓ* Chee	Penis	
ℓℓ Da	Slave	=	*ℓℓℓ* Daa	Rough surface	
ℓℓ Dam	Bamboo mat	=	*ℓℓℓ* Damm	Careless	
ℓℓ Di	Shield	=	*ℓℓ* Dee	Die	
ℓℓ Ga	Useless	=	*ℓℓℓ* Gaa	Afraid/Fear	
ℓℓ Gan	Fence	=	*ℓℓℓ* Gann	Shame	
ℓℓ Gi	Cane	=	*ℓℓ* Gee	Thread	
ℓℓ Gong	Horn	=	*ℓℓ* Gonng	Strong	
ℓℓ Go*	Bamboo	=	*ℓℓℓ* Go:*	Discussion/ Meeting	

---

* symbol shows incomplete pronunciation
Glottal Stops, IPA symbol 'ʔ' is used in English and Colon [:] is used in Hindi

Wancho		English	=	Wancho		English
	No*	Basket	=		No*	Turning
	Ni	Smile	=		Nee	Cloths
	Pan	Tree	=		Pann	Rule
	Pi	Fly	=		Pee	Bend
	Tu	Not sharp	=		Too	See
	Than	Face	=		Thann	Target
	Ki	Quarrel	=		Kee	Chick comes out of egg
	O	Noise	=		O	Bird
	Man	No	=		Mann	Name
	Khan	Yam	=		Khann	Buried
	Mai	Good	=		Maie	Animals/Meat
	Ja*	Water	=		Ja*	Bone
	Nga	Tire	=		Ngaa	Mithun
	Khi	Red	=		Khee	Keen
	Kan	To carry	=		Kann	Hug
	Kom	They	=		Komm	We
	Ju	Beg	=		Joo	Wine
	Pong	Meet	=		Pongn	Join
	Lam	Way	=		Lamm	seek/search
	Shan	Face	=		Shann	Praise
	Chuu	Bite	=		Chu	Melt

*** symbol shows incomplete pronunciation**
Glottal Stops, IPA symbol 'ʔ' is used in English and Colon [:] is used in Hindi

12 SENTENCES

English:	Wancho:	Translation in Wancho using Roman alphabet
Welcome.	𑢵𑣜𑣎\𑣕 𑣕𑣜𑣒𑣟𑣜𑣎	Maile paihai.
	𑢵𑣜𑣎\𑣕 𑣕𑣜𑣒𑣏𑣜𑣎	Maile paikai.
	𑢵𑣜𑣎\𑣕 𑣟𑣜𑣒𑣟𑣜𑣎	Maile ngoihai.
	𑢵𑣜𑣎 𑢵𑣜𑣎 𑟵𑣒𑣎 𑣟𑣜𑣎	Mai mai ngoi kai
Come here.	𑣜𑢵𑣜 𑣕𑣜𑣒𑣏𑣜𑣎	Ama paikai.
	𑣎𑢵𑣜 𑣕𑣜𑣒𑣟𑣜𑣎	Imma paihai.
Good.	𑢵𑣜𑣎𑣛𑣜	Maiga.
	𑢵𑣜𑣎𑣕𑣙	Maipu.
	𑢵𑣜𑣎\𑣕	Maile
How are you?	𑢵𑣜𑣎 𑢵𑣜𑣎 𑟵𑣜𑣕𑣟𑣜?	Mai mai taiza?
	𑢵𑣜𑣎 𑢵𑣜𑣎 𑟵𑣜𑣕𑣎𑟵𑣜?	Mai mai taicha?
	𑢵𑣜𑣎 𑢵𑣜𑣎 𑟵𑣜𑣎 𑣙𑣜?	Mai mai tai sha?
What is your name?	𑣘𑣛 𑣙\𑣕 𑢵𑣘?	Nang bale man?
	𑣘𑣛 𑢵𑣘 𑣜𑣙?	Nang man au?
	𑣘𑣛 𑢵𑣘 𑣒𑣟𑣜?	Nang man ova?
My name is Wangsu.	𑣏𑣙 𑢵𑣘 𑟱𑣛𑣜𑣙.	Kuman Wangsu.
	𑣏𑣒𑣎 𑢵𑣘 𑟱𑣛𑣜𑣙.	Koiman Wangsu.
	𑣏𑣙 𑟱𑣛𑣜𑣙 𑣜𑢵𑣜\𑣕.	Ku Wangsu amanle
I love you.	𑣏𑣙𑣕𑣕 𑣜𑣛𑟵𑣒𑣒 𑣒𑣜\𑣕.	Kuye nangto kanle.
	𑣏𑣙𑣕𑣕 𑣜𑣛𑟵𑣒𑣒 \𑣒\𑣕.	Kuye nangto lungle.

English:	Wancho:	Translation in Wancho using Roman alphabet
Thank you.	𑱲𑱲𑱲𑱲	Maiga.
	𑱲𑱲𑱲	Maile.
	𑱲𑱲𑱲𑱲	Maipu.
Best of luck.	𑱲𑱲𑱲𑱲𑱲	Namphoisu.
	𑱲𑱲𑱲𑱲𑱲	Nyemphoisu.
God bless you	𑱲𑱲𑱲𑱲𑱲	Phuhsumgang.
	𑱲𑱲𑱲𑱲𑱲	Phuhsumjang.
	𑱲𑱲𑱲𑱲𑱲	Phuhsumrang.
Please give me a glass of water.	𑱲𑱲 𑱲𑱲 𑱲𑱲	Ti tapha hai.
	𑱲𑱲 𑱲𑱲 𑱲𑱲𑱲𑱲	Kuang ti songpha hai.
	𑱲𑱲𑱲 𑱲𑱲 𑱲𑱲 𑱲𑱲	Koiya chi chepha kai.

13 NUMERALS

---

0. O   = Zero

1. ℒ   = 𝒸𝓏(Ta ता), 𝓏𝒸𝓏(Ata अता),

          𝒻𝓏(Cha चा), 𝓏𝒻𝓏(Acha अचा), one

2. 9   = 𝓏∠Z(Ani अनी), Two

3. Ɑ   = 𝓏ꞓ℃(Ajam अजम), 𝓏𝒫℃(Adam अदम),

          𝓏⅃℃(Aram अरम), Three

4. ♂   = 𝓏∖Z(Ali अली), 𝒷ꞓZ(Bazi बजी), Four

5. ♂   = 𝓏Ϭ𝓏(Aga अगा), 𝓏𝒫𝓏(Anga अड ा),

          𝓏℃𝒷𝓏(Anya अज्ञा), Five

6. ?   = 𝓏ꞓꞛ(Azok अजोक), 𝓏⅃ꞛ(Arok अरोक),

          𝓏Ϭꞛ(Agok अगोक), Six

7. V   = 𝓏∠𝒹(Anat अनत), Seven

8. ♂   = 𝓏𝒻𝒹(Achat अचत),

          𝓏ℒ𝒹(Asat असत), Eight

9. ℀   = 𝓏ꞛ℣(Aku अकु), Nine

TABLE

TABLE

ᚁᚂ	ᚁᚂ	ᚁᚂ	ᚁᚂ	ᚁᚂ

SIGNS: Operator Symbols

Signs and symbols of the counting numbers is same as used in English such as (+), (-), (x), (/), (=), (%), and decimal (.) etc.

COUNTING NUMBERS

1.0	= BAN
9O	= TA, TSHA
2.0	= TABAN, TSHABAN
ƆO	= PUNI, PANYI
ȥO	= PUNIBAN, PANYIBAN
ʔO	= PURAM, PUJAM, PARAM
VO	= PURAMBAN, PUJAMBAN
ᵺO	= PUBAZI, PALI
ᵹO	= PUBAZIBAN, PALIBAN
1.00	= HOCHA, HOTA
9OO	= HO-ANI
2.00	= HO-ARAM, HO-AZAM
ƆOO	= HO-BAZI, HO-ALI
ȥOO	= HO-ANYA, HO-ANGA, HO-AGA
ʔOO	= HO-AGOK, HO-AZOK, HO-AROK
VOO	= HO-ANAT
ᵺOO	= HO-ASAT, HO-ACHAT
ᵹOO	= HO-AKU
1.000	= JAATCHA, JAATTA
9OOO	= JAAT ANI
2.000	= JAAT ARAM, JAAT AZAM
ƆOOO	= JAAT BAZI, JAAT ALI
ȥOOO	= JAAT ANYA, JAAT ANGA
ʔOOO	= JAAT AGOK, JAAT AZOK
VOOO	= JAAT ANAT
ᵺOOO	= JAAT ASAT, JAAT ACHAT
ᵹOOO	= JAAT AKU
1.0000	= JAAT BAN

9OOOO	= JAAT TA, JAAT TSHA
2OOOO	= JAAT ARAM, JAAT AZAM
ꝑOOOO	= JAAT BAZI, JAAT BALI
ꝑOOOO	= JAAT ANYA, JAAT ANGA
ꝒOOOO	= JAAT AGOK, JAAT AZOK
VOOOO	= JAAT ANAT
ꝼOOOO	= JAAT ASAT, JAAT ACHAT
ꝁOOOO	= JAAT AKU
1OOOOO	= LAKH CHA, LAKH TAA
9OOOOO	= LAKH ANI
2OOOOO	= LAKH ARAM, LAKH AZAM
ꝑOOOOO	= LAKH BAZI, LAKH ALI
ꝑOOOOO	= LAKH ANYA, LAKH AGA, LAKH ANGA
ꝒOOOOO	= LAKH AGOK, LAKH AZOK, LAKH AROK
VOOOOO	= LAKH ANAT
ꝼOOOOO	= LAKH ASAT, LAKH ACHAT
ꝁOOOOO	= LAKH AKU
1OOOOOO	= LAKH BAN
9OOOOOO	= LAKH TA, LAKH TSHA
2OOOOOO	= LAKH TABAN, LAKH TSHABAN
ꝑOOOOOO	= LAKH PUNI, LAKH PALI
ꝑOOOOOO	= LAKH PUNIBAN, LAKH PANYI BAN
ꝒOOOOOO	= LAKH PURAM, LAKH PUJAM, LAKH PARAM
VOOOOOO	= LAKH PURAM BAN, LAKH PUJAM BAN
ꝼOOOOOO	= LAKH PUBAZI, LAKH PALI
ꝁOOOOOO	= LAKH PUBAZIBAN, LAKH PALIBAN
1OOOOOOO	= CRORE CHA, CRORE TAA

ADDITION
৭ඦ𝒵ไ৯/ℒඦ𝒵ไ৯

Addition Examples given below:

(a) $\text{ঌ} + \text{৯} = \text{ไJ}$

(b) $\text{𝒇} + V = \text{ไঌ}$

(c) $\text{৯} + V = \text{ไP}$

(d) $\text{ไ } \Omega + J = \text{ไV}$

(e) $\text{ไ } \text{ঌ} + \Omega = \text{ไ𝒇}$

(i).

$$\begin{array}{cccc} V & \text{৯P} & \text{𝒇 J P} & \text{9 0 } \Omega \text{ ไ} \\ +\ J & +\ \text{ไ৯} & +\ 9\ \text{𝒇} & +\ \text{𝒇 9 } V \\ \hline \text{ไไ ,} & \text{ไไঌ .} & \text{𝒇 } V\ J\ . & \text{9 𝒇 ঌ 𝒇 .} \end{array}$$

(ii).

$$\begin{array}{cccc} \text{𝒇 J 𝒇} & \text{P } \Omega\ J & \text{P } J\ V\ \text{ঌ} & \text{৯ P } \Omega\ \text{𝒇} \\ +\ J\ \text{ঌ} & +\ V\ J & +\ \text{𝒇 9 } \Omega & +\ J\ V\ \text{ไ} \\ +\ \text{ไ 0} & +\ 9\ 0 & +\ \Omega\ 0\ 0 & +\ J\ \text{ঌ P} \\ \hline \text{৯ 0 } \Omega & V\ 9\ \text{𝒇} & V\ \text{ঌ ৯ 𝒇} & \text{ไ 0 ঌ P ঌ} \end{array}$$

SUBTRACTION

Examples:

(a) .　　　　　　　𝑘 – ᘆ　　=　ᖳ

(b) .　　　　　　　𝑓 – 𝑔　　=　ᘆ

(c) .　　　　　ᖷ ᘆ – 𝑔 𝑗　=　–𝑙𝑙

(d) .　　　　　𝑓 0 – 𝑔 𝑓　=　𝑔𝑔

(i).　　　𝑘 ᖳ ᘆ 𝑉 𝑓　　　𝑓 𝑔 𝑉 𝑗 ᖳ　　　𝑉 ᖷ ᖳ 𝑔 𝑓
　　　 – ᘆ 𝑓 𝑔 0　　　 – ᘆ 𝑓 𝑔 ᖷ　　　 – 𝑗 𝑓 ᖳ 𝑘
　　　　𝑘 𝑔 𝑓 𝑓 𝑓　　　 𝑉 𝑘 𝑔 𝑔 𝑓　　　 ᖳ ᖳ 𝑉 𝑓 ᖳ

(ii).　　 𝑓 𝑘 𝑉 ᘆ ᖳ　　 𝑘 𝑘 𝑓 𝑓 0　　 𝑘 𝑘 𝑘 𝑘 𝑘
　　　 – ᘆ 𝑉 𝑓 𝑘　　 – 𝑔 ᖳ ᘆ 𝑉　　 – ᖳ 0 𝑓 𝑉
　　　　𝑓 𝑓 𝑘 𝑗 𝑉　　 𝑘 𝑉 𝑔 𝑗 ᘆ　　 𝑘 ᘆ 𝑘 𝑗 𝑔

MULTIPLICATION

Examples:

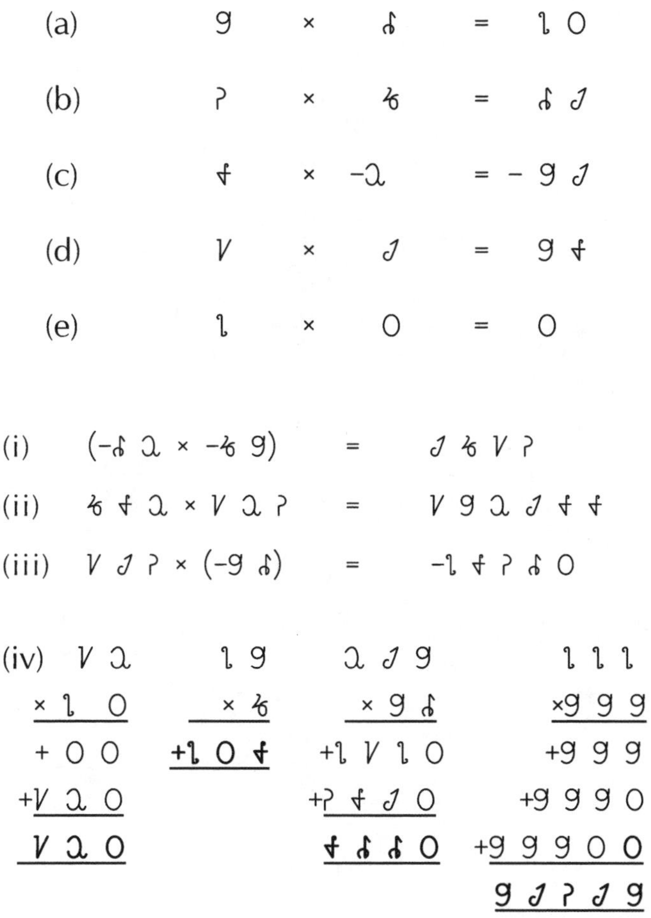

(a) 9 × ♪ = �welve O

(b) ? × ⅙ = ♪ ♩

(c) ⨍ × −Ϩ = − 9 ♩

(d) V × ♩ = 9 ⨍

(e) ⒈ × O = O

(i) (−♪ Ϩ × −⅙ 9) = ♩ ⅙ V ?

(ii) ⅙ ⨍ Ϩ × V Ϩ ? = V 9 Ϩ ♩ ⨍ ⨍

(iii) V ♩ ? × (−9 ♪) = −⒈ ⨍ ? ♪ O

(iv)
V Ϩ	⒈ 9	Ϩ ♩ 9	⒈ ⒈ ⒈
× ⒈ O	× ⅙	× 9 ♪	×9 9 9
+ O O	+⒈ O ⨍	+⒈ V ⒈ O	+9 9 9
+V Ϩ O		+? ⨍ ♩ O	+9 9 9 O
V Ϩ O		⨍ ♪ ♪ O	+9 9 9 O O
			9 ♩ ? ♩ 9

DIVISION

Examples:

(a) 9 𝒥 ÷ 9 = ꞁ 9

(b) ꜰ ? ÷ V = ꜰ

(c) ꜰ ? V ÷ ꜰ 𝒥 = ꞁ?. O?

(d) −9 ꜰ O ÷ ꜰ = −ꜰO

(e) ꞁ 9 ꝏ 𝒥 ꜰ ? V ꜰ ⅍ ÷ ⅍⅍⅍ = ꞁ9ꝏ.ꜰO.ꝏ?⅍ꝏV

(i)
$$
\begin{array}{r}
\mathcal{J}V\Omega\delta \\
\hline
\mathcal{ꞁ9}\ )\ \overline{\delta?ꜰ9?} \\
-\mathcal{J}ꜰ \\
\hline
ꜰꜰ \\
-ꜰ\mathcal{J} \\
\hline
\mathcal{J}9 \\
-\Omega? \\
\hline
?\ ? \\
-?O \\
\hline
?
\end{array}
$$

(ii)
$$
\begin{array}{r}
\mathcal{J}O \\
\hline
\delta\ )\ \overline{9OO} \\
-9O \\
\hline
OO \\
-O \\
\hline
O
\end{array}
$$

Remainder

14 DAYS, MONTHS & YEAR

DAYS IN A WEEK

English	Pronounciation		Wancho
Sunday	Nansa	न्नसा	ᘒᘔᘒᘔ
Monday	Nihcha	निःचा	ᘔᘓᘕᘔ
Tuesday	Nihani	निःअनी	ᘔᘓᘔᘒᘔ
Wednesday	Niharam	निःअरम	ᘔᘓᘔᘕᘖ
Thursday	Nihbezi	निःबजी	ᘔᘓᘔᘕᘔ
Friday	Nihanya	निःअजया	ᘔᘓᘔᘔᘕᘔ
Saturday	Nihagok	निःअगोक	ᘔᘓᘔᘔᘕᘔ

DAY IN A MONTH

1.	𑯁𑯚𑯔𑯌𑯚	Ngaisa	ङाईसा
2.	𑯚𑯎𑯔	Ani	अनी
3.	𑯚𑯟𑯐	Adam	अदम
4.	𑯟𑯙𑯔	Bezi	बजी
5.	𑯚𑯈𑯌𑯚	Anya	अज्ञा
6.	𑯚𑯔𑯏	Agok	अगोक
7.	𑯚𑯎𑯠	Anat	अनत
8.	𑯚𑯌𑯠	Asat	असत
9.	𑯚𑯓𑯕	Aku	अकू
10.	𑯟𑯎𑯎	Ba:n	बन
11.	𑯗𑯈𑯌𑯚	Lomsa	लोमसा
12.	𑯗𑯈𑯎𑯕	Lomnu	लोमनू
13.	𑯍𑯔𑯎	Jon	जोन
14.	𑯕𑯚𑯚𑯎	Taan	तान
15.	𑯘𑯏𑯌𑯚	Nyeaksa	ञेकसा

16.	ᤄᤔᤗᤢ	Nyeaknu	ञेकनू
17.	ᤄᤔᤕᤏᤗ	Nyeak ngan	ञेकङान
18.	ᤐᤗᤢ-੨	Khai-III	खई – III
19.	ᤐᤗᤢ-ᤀ	Khai-IV	खई – IV
20.	ᤐᤗᤢ-ᤄ	Khai-V	खई – V
21.	ᤐᤗᤢ-ᤇ	Khai-VI	खई – VI
22.	ᤐᤗᤢ-V	Khai-VII	खई – VII
23.	ᤐᤗᤢ-ᤵ	Khai-VIII	खई – VIII
24.	ᤐᤗᤢ-ᤀ	Khai-IX	खई – IX
25.	ᤐᤗᤢ-੧0	Khai-X	खई – X
26.	ᤏᤩᤢ	Oju	ओजु
27.	ᤗᤗᤢᤗᤏ	Laipam	लाईपम
28.	ᤖᤢᤗᤗ	Gunn	गून
29.	ᤄᤗᤗ	Mann	मन
30.	ᤑᤏᤣ-ᤏ	Joh-o	जोःओ
31.	ᤑᤏᤗᤄᤏᤣ	Jenmah	जेनमाः

MONTHS IN A YEAR

English	Wancho	Pronounciation	
January	𞋲𞋛𞋩𞋞𞋦	Painu	पाईनू
February	𞋒𞋁𞋞𞋦	Changnu	चंनू
March	𞋃𞋞𞋞𞋦	Kannu	कन्नू
April	𞋒𞋫𞋃𞋞𞋦	Diknu	दिकनू
May	𞋒𞋫𞋃𞋛𞋩	Diksa	दिकसा
June	𞋒𞋩𞋩𞋞𞋦	Teenu	तनू
July	𞋞𞋛𞋞𞋞𞋦	Nannu	नान्नू
August	𞋒𞋦𞋞𞋦	Dunu	डूनू
September	𞋡𞋡𞋛𞋞𞋦	Hohanu	होहानू
October	𞋞𞋒𞋞𞋦	Naumnu	नमनू
November	𞋒𞋒𞋞𞋦	Chamnu	चमनू
December	𞋒𞋞𞋞𞋦	Ngannu	ङन्नू

Ref: Mr. Phawang Wangham of Kamhua Noknu Village.

15 NAME OF THE WANCHO VILLAGES

Pongchau & Wakka Circle

1.	ᢩᠸᠵᠸ	Patau (Pongchau)HQ	प्ताउ/पोंचौ
2.	ᡞᠸᠵᠵᠵᢩ	Nyahngo (Bonia)	ञाःङो/बोञा
3.	ᠬᠸᠸ ᠸᢩ	Konnu	कोन्नू
4.	ᠬᠸᠸᠵᠵ	Konsa	कोनसा
5.	ᠵᠼᠵᠵ	Khasa	खंसा
6.	ᠵᠼᠵᠸ	Jangan (Jagan)	जंङन/जगान
7.	ᠵᠼᠸᢩ	Khanu	खंनू
8.	ᠸᠸᠸᢩ	Gotnu (Votnu)	गोतनू/वोतनू
9.	ᠬᠵᠼᠸᠵᠵ ᠸᠬᠸᢩ	Kamhua Noknu	कामहों नोकनू
10.	ᠬᠵᠼᠸᠵᠵ ᠸᠬᠵᠵ	Kamhua Noksa	कामहों नोकसा
11.	ᠬᠵᠼᠸᠸᠹ	Kampong	कामपों
12.	ᠹᠸᠸ	Chop	चोप
13.	ᠸᠬᠵᠬᠵᠵ	Gakkah (Wakka)HQ.	गक्काः/वक्काः
14.	ᠹᠹᠵᠵ	Chongkho	चोंखो
15.	ᠸᠵᠵᠵ	Ngisa	नीसा
16.	ᠸᠵᠸᢩ	Nginu	नीनू
17.	ᠸᠹᠬᠵᠵ	Longkai	लोंकई
18.	ᠵᠸᠸᠸᠵ	Khogla	खोकःला
19.	ᠬᠵᠵᠸᠵᠵ	Kaimoi	काइमोइ
20.	ᠬᠵᠵᠸᠵᠵ	Kaiho	काइहों

Longding & Pamau Circle

1.	𞋲𞋩𞋛𞋚𞋩	Pumau HQ	पुमाउ
2.	𞋛𞋜𞋝𞋞𞋛	Niahlam (Longkhau)	ज्याःलम / लोंखाउ
3.	𞋟𞋚𞋛𞋠	Chatting	चातीं
4.	𞋛𞋜𞋝𞋩𞋛𞋚	Maihua	माइहोया
5.	𞋛𞋚𞋩𞋛𞋚	Niausa	न्याउसा
6.	𞋛𞋚𞋩𞋜𞋩	Niaunu	न्याउनू
7.	𞋛𞋜𞋟𞋠	Michong (Mintong)	मिचों / मिनतों
8.	𞋩𞋠𞋒𞋠	Longphong	लोंफों
9.	𞋟𞋜𞋩𞋚	Zedua	जेदूआ
10.	𞋚𞋜𞋛𞋩𞋚	Senua	सेनुआ
11.	𞋚𞋜𞋛𞋩𞋚 𞋜𞋝𞋚𞋚	Senua Noksa	सिज्ञूआ नोकसा
12.	𞋟𞋚𞋜𞋚	Tissa	तिसा
13.	𞋙𞋜𞋟𞋜𞋚𞋜	Hahnan (Tissa Camp)	हाःनान / तिसाकेम
14.	𞋩𞋠𞋒𞋠	Longding HQ	लोंदिड.
15.	𞋩𞋠𞋚𞋠𞋛	Longsom	लोंसोम
16.	𞋟𞋚𞋜𞋩	Chanu	चॉनू
17.	𞋙𞋚𞋚𞋛𞋙	Ozakho	अजाखो
18.	𞋟𞋚𞋠𞋠	Chatong	चातों

Kannubari & Launu Circle

1.	༡༦༦༦	Olingtong	अलिंतों
2.	༠௯௫	Wan	वानू
3.	༢௯௫௯	Russ	रुसा
4.	௯௯ ௯௯௯௯ ௯௯௯	Hahsia Russa	हाःसया रुसा
5.	௯௯௯௯	Chopsa	चोपसा
6.	௯௯௫௫	Chopnu	चोपनू
7.	௯௫௯௫	Ranglua	रंलोअ
8.	௯௯௯௯௯	Otongkhua	ओतोंखोआ
9.	௫௫௯௯	Naitong	नाईतों
10.	௯௫௯௫	Launu	लाउनू
11.	௯௯௫௫௫௯	Mopakhat	मोपाखात
12.	௯௯௫௯	Longhua	लोंहोअ
13.	௯௫௫௫௫௫	Kanubari HQ.	कानूबारी
14.	௯௫௫௫௫	Luaksim	लुअक्सिम
15.	௯௯௫௯	Kamkuh Russa	कमकुः
16.	௫௫௯௫௫௯	Dahsatong	डाःसातों
17.	௫௫௫௯௫௫	Banfera	बनफेरा
18.	௯௯௫௫௫	Longnakse	लोंनकसे
19.	௯௫௯௫	Kamnu	क्मनू
20.	௫௯௫௫	Nokfan	नोकफन
21.	௯௯௫௯௫௫	Longkhojan	लोंखोजान
22.	௯௫௫௫௯	Ngamding	ङामदीङ
23.	௯௯௫௫	Ringpong	रिङपं
24.	௫௫௫௯	Tewai	तिवाई
25.	௫௫௯௯	Tissing	तिसीङ
26.	௫௫௫௫௯	Sangsathong	संसाथों

Longding Circle

S. No	Total Rural/Urban	No of Households	Persons	Males	Females
1	Total	2,691	15,703	8,239	7,464
2	Rural	2,691	15,703	8,239	7,464
3	Urban	0	0	0	0

Village Details of   Longding Circle

S.No	Town/ Village Name	No of Households	Persons	Males	Females
1	Chanu	189	1,218	597	621
2	Chattong	59	344	169	175
3	Longding H.Q.	795	3,615	2,069	1,546
4	Longphong	161	1,070	520	550
5	Longsom	137	912	441	471
6	Mintong	183	1,250	622	628
7	Niaunu	246	1,448	709	739
8	Niausa	239	1,716	940	776
9	Ozakho	84	555	281	274
10	Senua	206	1,345	663	682
11	Senua Noksa	50	267	140	127
12	Senua S.T.C. Camp	31	83	49	34
13	Tissa Camp	213	1,083	641	442

Pongchau Circle

S. No	Total Rural/Urban	No of Households	Persons	Males	Females
1	Total	1,688	10,421	5,407	5,014
2	Rural	1,688	10,421	5,407	5,014
3	Urban	0	0	0	0

Village Details of   Pongchau Circle

S.No	Town Village Name	No of Households	Persons	Males	Females
1	Bonia	133	897	453	444
2	Jagan	95	649	344	305
3	Kamhua Noknu	218	1,357	711	646
4	Kamhua Noksa	128	769	380	389
5	Khasa	208	1,283	658	625
6	Konnu	185	1,080	535	545
7	Konsa	122	698	353	345
8	Lower Pongchau	116	786	411	375
9	Pongchau	218	1,513	789	724
10	Pongchau H.Q.	168	750	458	292
11	Votnu	97	639	315	324

Population Data collected, based on Population Census of India 2001

Pumao Circle

S. No	Total Rural/Urban	No of Households	Persons	Males	Females
1	Total	574	4,312	2,232	2,080
2	Rural	574	4,312	2,232	2,080
3	Urban	0	0	0	0
	Village Details of	Pumao Circle			

S.No	Town Village Name	No of Households	Persons	Males	Females
1	Chatting	113	889	469	420
2	Longkhaw	200	1,596	812	784
3	Maihua	54	356	203	153
4	Pumao	192	1,427	722	705
5	Pumao H.Q.	15	44	26	18

Wakka Circle

S. No	Total Rural/Urban	No of Households	Persons	Males	Females
1	Total	1,605	9,246	4,730	4,516
2	Rural	1,605	9,246	4,730	4,516
3	Urban	0	0	0	0
	Village Details of	Wakka Circle			

S.No	Town Village Name	No of Households	Persons	Males	Females
1	Chongkho	93	653	316	337
2	Chop	49	316	160	156
3	Kaimoi	112	632	348	284
4	Kampong	15	96	51	45
5	Khanu	244	1,346	693	653
6	Khogla	97	597	318	279
7	Longkai	131	721	351	370
8	Lower Nginu	222	1,143	588	555
9	Nginu	132	777	382	395
10	Ngisa	104	712	351	361
11	Wakka	298	1,806	908	898
12	Wakka H.Q.	108	447	264	183

Population Data collected, based on Population Census of India 2001

Kanubari Circle

S. No	Total Rural/Urban	No of Households	Persons	Males	Females
1	Total	1,965	11,340	5,839	5,501
2	Rural	1,965	11,340	5,839	5,501
3	Urban	0	0	0	0
	Village Details of	Kanubari Circle			

S.No	Town/Village Name	No of Households	Persons	Males	Females
1	Banfera	136	1,033	536	497
2	Chopnu	127	847	396	451
3	Chopsa	53	326	160	166
4	Dasatong	116	643	329	314
5	Hasse Russa	93	508	273	235
6	Kamku Russa	60	270	138	132
7	Kamnu	18	106	43	63
8	Kanubari H.Q.	268	1,111	595	516
9	Laonu	36	222	123	99
10	Longhua	84	577	313	264
11	Longkhojan	20	105	51	54
12	Luaksim	84	503	250	253
13	Mopakhat	150	803	422	381
14	Naitong	47	296	152	411
15	Ngamding	6	27	14	13
16	Nokfan	65	399	203	196
17	Olingtong	127	646	344	302
18	Otonghkhua	75	416	194	222
19	Ranglua	153	751	399	352
20	Ringpong	4	16	8	8
21	Russa	71	445	247	198
22	Sang Sathong	14	88	40	48
23	Tewai	4	8	8	0
24	Tissing	4	12	8	4
25	Wanu	150	1,182	593	589

Names of Wancho Speaking Villages outside Longding District

Tirap District

1. Lapnan
2. Lothong
3. Chasa
4. Longo
5. Lower Kamhua

Nagaland State

1. Nokjan
2. Jangkham
3. Longwa
4. Phumching
5. Pukha
6. Longgo
7. Watting
8. Jansa
9. Old Jansa
10. Nokdang
11. Tangnu
12. Sangnu
13. Nyahnu
14. Gamsa
15. Sahah Tingnu
16. Sahah Gamsa
17. Sahah Tangchen

18. Yuching
19. Dahsa
20. Mon
21. Longphoh
22. Sahah Lampong
23. Oting
24. Lapa Lampong
25. Lapa
26. Lokun
27. Chi
28. Totok
29. Totok Tingnu
30. Totok Tingkho
31. Totok Tingha
32. Longkai
33. Lohah
34. Chingtang
35. Tanhai
36. Aboi
37. Tamlu
38. Lokhua
39. Hahse Namsa

Still to be recognized many villages

Burma

1. Kamkah
2. Chuja
3. Longpa
4. Chopkhaw

5. Khamngoi
6. Longkai
7. Thajup
8. Langoi
9. Nahsa
10. Thala
11. Longkai

12. Momkho
13. Orok Noksa

14. Loiji
15. Langkhaw

16. Papong
17. Jordong
18. Gaktham
19. Gosoi
20. Khajo(Khamlau)
21. Phumching
22. Longpa
23. Maidongching

Bhutan

1. Paro (prince habitation)
2. Haa (capital Town)
3. Dukhijong

Assam

1. Goriabam (Near Namrup)
2. Longtcha (Near Namrup)
3. Deopani (Near Namrup)
4. Baregoan (Near Kanubari)

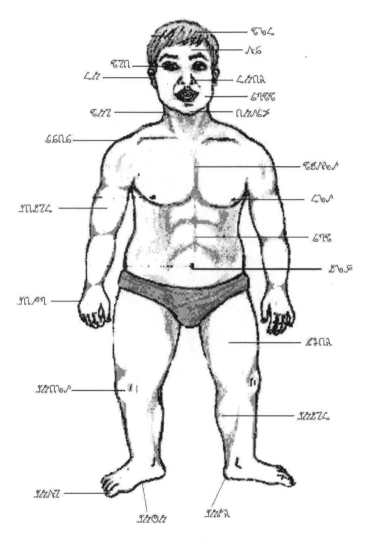

Figure 12

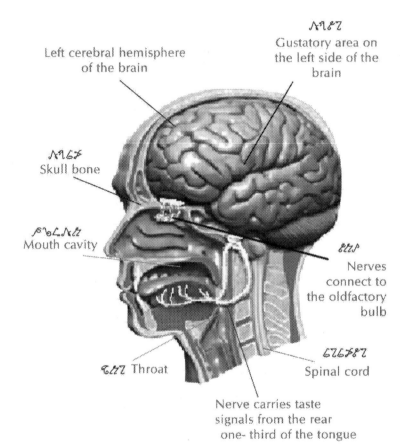

ᝬᝁᝨ᝵
Gustatory area on
the left side of the
brain

Left cerebral hemisphere
of the brain

ᝬᝁᝬ᝵
Skull bone

ᝡᝳᝲᝲᝨᝬ
Mouth cavity

ᝨᝨ᝵
Nerves
connect to
the oldfactory
bulb

ᝲᝨᝲ᝵ᝨ᝵
Spinal cord

ᝨᝨ᝵ Throat

Nerve carries taste
signals from the rear
one- third of the tongue

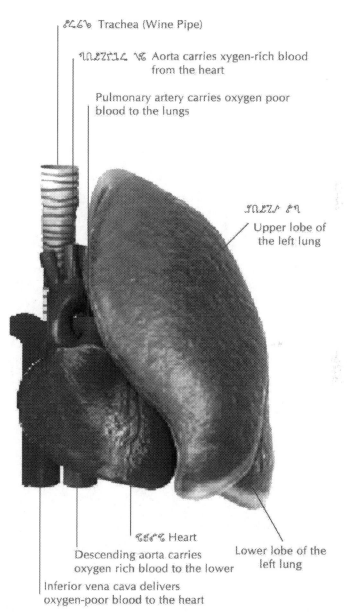

ᏁᏓᎬ Trachea (Wine Pipe)

ᏗᏁᏍᏗᏟ Ꮴ Aorta carries xygen-rich blood
from the heart

Pulmonary artery carries oxygen poor
blood to the lungs

ᏃᏁᏍᏚ ᏋᏁ
Upper lobe of
the left lung

ᏋᏍᎷᏋ Heart

Descending aorta carries
oxygen rich blood to the lower

Lower lobe of the
left lung

Inferior vena cava delivers
oxygen-poor blood to the heart

Figure 14

ᛒᚱ Skull

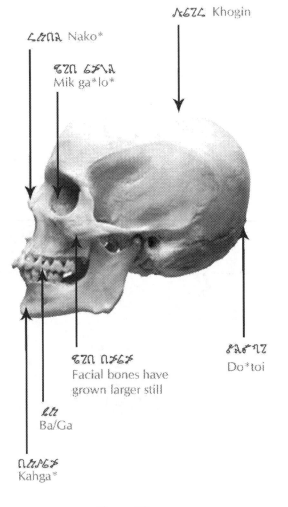

ᛩᛒᛉᛚ Khogin

ᒪᛒᚿᛩ Nako*

ᛖᛉᚿ ᛒᛣᛚᛩ
Mik ga*lo*

ᛖᛉᚿ ᚿᛣᛒᛣ
Facial bones have
grown larger still

ᛩᛩᛒᛖ ᛚᛉ
Do*toi

ᛒᛩ
Ba/Ga

ᚿᛖᛉᛣ
Kahga*

Figure 15

* symbol shows incomplete pronunciation and colon [:] is used as a glottal stop which is
compared to symbol 'ʔ' in IPA

HUMAN BRAIN

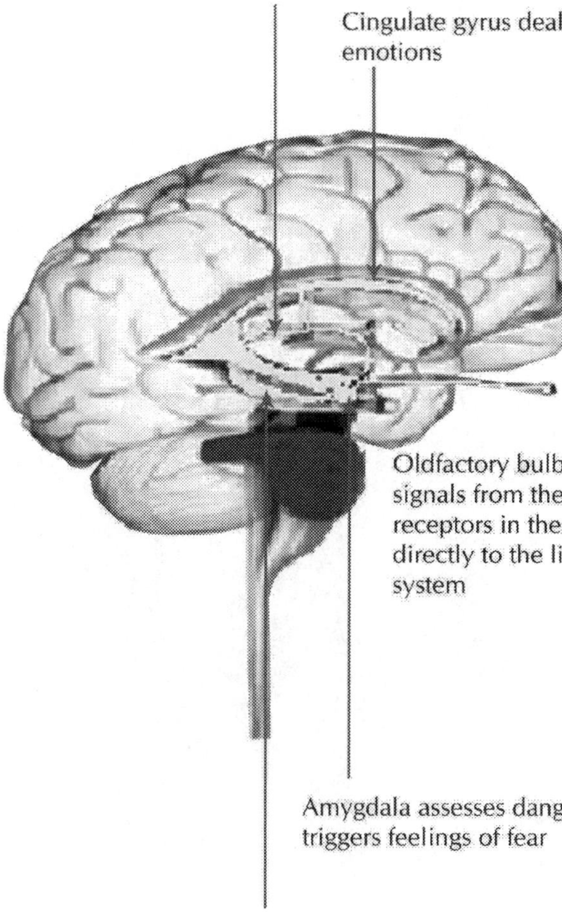

ᐱᕿᑐᑕ ᐱᖑᕉᖧᖬᕿ

Fornix is the pathhway that links
different parts of the limbic system

Cingulate gyrus deals with
emotions

Oldfactory bulbs carry
signals from the smell
receptors in the nose
directly to the limbic
system

Amygdala assesses danger and
triggers feelings of fear

Hippocampus deals with memory
and navigation

Figure 16

KIDNEY

The kidneys filter the blood to remove wastes and extra water and salts. The liver is a chemical factory that does more than 500 different jobs, including the processing of food and the removal of wastes from the blood.

Each kidney has about a million tiny filters, which between them clean about a quarter of your blood every minute. The unwanted substances combine with water to make urine, which trickles down to the bladder.

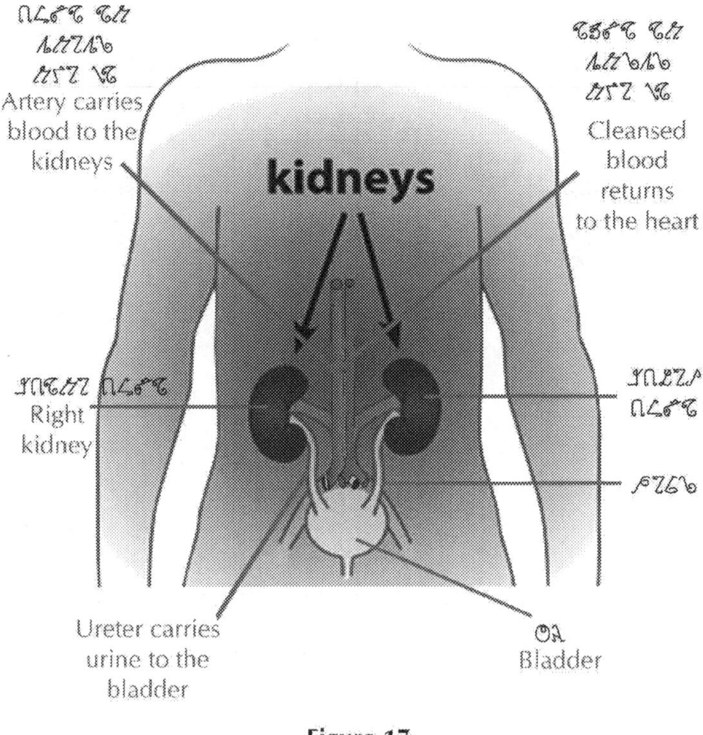

Figure 17

Figure 18

ꫛ for Ngun = ꫛ

ꫛꦫꦊ(Ngun) = Money

ꫛ = Rs/$/

So, We can write Rs. 1000.00 as ꫛ. 1000.00

17 POEMS & SONGS

According to Oxford Advanced Dictionary 'poem is a piece of writing in which the words are chosen for their sound and the images they suggest, not just for their obvious meanings. The words are arranged in separate lines, usually with a repeated rhythm, and often the lines RHYME at the end'. Poetry has always been a source of inspiration for mankind. Ideas of poetry have a natural appeal as they reflects the inner most emotions of humans. Poetry is also an art that cut across all barriers.

William Wordsworth has defined poetry as "The spontaneous overflow of powerful feelings arising from emotions recollected in tranquility". Many poets and poetess become a favorite and lover of mankind fascinated by their poetic words entere into the deepest part of heart with imaginations and feelings. Such poetic words of Wanchos are very interesting and heart touching which creates the emotional feelings of man and brings imaginations alive in front of our eyes. Some of the poetic words of Wancho are, 'Po (Tree), Ja (Water), Seynu (Sun), etc.' These are used only as poetic language and not in formal or common language. Wanchos are creative by nature they can capture the heart of million people through writing poems, using poetic words into verse of the poem. Poem can be written in any language so, Wanchos are encouraged to write in their own language like Rabindranath Tagore, Indian poet who wrote Gitanjali, "Offering of Songs" in Bengali . He was awarded the Nobel prize at the time of Irish poet Yeats, who was the most prominent poet in England in those days. Here, some poems have been taken from my collections in next pages.

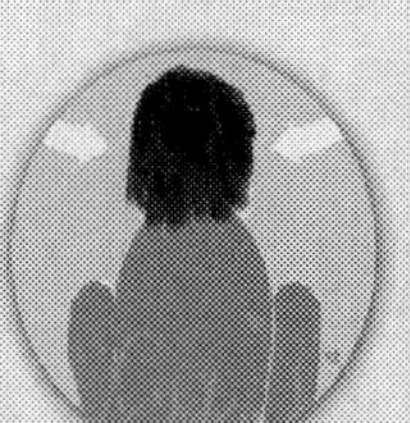

Recall the Days those Pleasant Days
(Translated in English)

Recall the days those pleasant days
Received your letter hid to friends,
Read it lonely whole heartedly keep it under pillow,
Take it out, read again and again thinking is it true or dreaming.

    Recall the days those pleasant days
    The day of first meet rapid my heart beat,
    Your nervous face sticks my eyes on!
    Stood silently talking nothing to other,
    Glance at a time ended with smiles.

Recall the days those pleasant days
The day of refusal when I hold you,
Your lovely fingers pinch my fort-arms,
The walk of evening on the promenade,
Your envisaging eyes tell the strength of love.

    Recall the days those pleasant days
    The day of last meet sharing of last word,
    Handover the beautiful gifts winded with threads of love,

    Shaking of burning hands lasting for half and hour,

    Rosy lip on my cheek, dropping tears on my toe.

    Recall the days those pleasant days.

New Moon

O, Dinosaur, Dragon...
        I too am coming soon, thy way
        Thou get ready; garland, aroma spray.

A message from above contained
The arrival of lifeless Omnivorous is certain.
Thou not heard the noise, breaking border wall?
Often my mind roved, I could know no savior to call.
Warns he that! "Love no living creature, any longer".
Nay! Started trips with ammo stronger,

The head and tail of the world can save no more
from being damaged.
Soon the earth will be swallowed, except dead
sands and stones.
If it's the will of father, life returns to the Stone Age.
If not so, thou need no worry, let's shine at night.
Another Armstrong will land on it and prove us right.

(This poem is an allegorical lyric depicting the extinction of
Dinosaurs and Dragon from the earth, due to the adverse climatic
condition of earth's atmosphere. Similarly, all the living creatures of
the earth including human-beings are going to be grasped by the
deadly radiation of Ultraviolet Ray arrived on the earth due to
depletion of ozone layer, makes Ozone hole. Hence, soon all the
living creatures are going to be extinct from the earth and, this earth
will be appeared like a moon. This poem is also published in "The
Peak-07", the Annual Magazine of Rajiv Gandhi Central University,
Doimuk, in the year 2007.)

MAIZA

ᨀᨈᨑᨕᨈ

ᨀᨈᨑᨕᨈ ᨀᨈᨑᨕᨈ ᨒᨐᨑ ᨀᨈᨑᨕᨈ?

   ᨀᨒᨀᨈᨐ ᨀᨒᨀᨈᨐ ᨒᨐᨑᨕᨏ ᨀᨒᨀᨈᨐ.

ᨀᨈᨑᨕᨈ ᨀᨈᨑᨕᨈ ᨏᨑᨒᨀᨈ ᨀᨈᨑᨕᨈ?

   ᨀᨒᨀᨈᨐ ᨀᨒᨀᨈᨐ ᨏᨑᨐᨀᨈ ᨀᨒᨀᨈᨐ.

ᨀᨈᨑᨕᨈ ᨀᨈᨑᨕᨈ ᨏᨐᨍᨐᨑ ᨀᨈᨑᨕᨈ?

   ᨀᨒᨀᨈᨐ ᨀᨒᨀᨈᨐ ᨕᨏᨐᨑ ᨀᨒᨀᨈᨐ.

ᨀᨈᨑᨕᨈ ᨀᨈᨑᨕᨈ ᨒᨕᨒ ᨀᨈᨑᨕᨈ?

   ᨀᨒᨀᨈᨐ ᨀᨒᨀᨈᨐ ᨒᨕᨒᨐᨑ ᨀᨒᨀᨈᨐ.

ᨀᨈᨑᨕᨈ ᨀᨈᨑᨕᨈ ᨕᨐᨑᨒᨏᨕᨒᨐᨑ ᨀᨈᨑᨕᨈ?

   ᨀᨈᨑᨒᨈ ᨀᨈᨑᨒᨈ ᨕᨐᨑᨒᨏᨕᨒᨐᨑ ᨀᨈᨑᨒᨈ.

ᨀᨈᨑᨕᨈ ᨀᨈᨑᨕᨈ ᨏᨏ ᨀᨈᨑᨐ ᨀᨈᨑᨕᨈ?

   ᨀᨈᨑᨒᨈ ᨀᨈᨑᨒᨈ ᨒᨏᨐᨕᨏ ᨒᨕᨒᨐ ᨀᨈᨑᨒᨈ.

ᨀᨈᨑᨕᨈ ᨀᨈᨑᨕᨈ ᨒᨑᨐᨏ ᨒᨕᨒᨐ ᨀᨈᨑᨕᨈ?

   ᨀᨈᨑᨒᨈ ᨀᨈᨑᨒᨈ ᨒᨑᨐᨏ ᨒᨕᨒᨐ ᨒᨏ ᨀᨈᨑᨒᨈ.

KOI GAGA

(Translated below)

Koi gaga O koi gaga
    Nuna kaong Pana kaong
Humto, koi gaga O koi gaga
    Apuna phawto Apeena hungto
Khungto, koi gaga O koi gaga
    Sampa na hatai Lamgoi na hatai
Chingto, koi gaga O koi gaga
    Sah na hatai jing na hatai
Maanphe, koi gaga O koi gaga.

A child is weeping, singing above song (Poem) with her toy horse (Maan) during the day at home. Her mother, father and parents went to field leaving her alone, no one was there to take care of and play with her except toy.

Definition in brief: The Poem is an elegy on the death soul, enquiring about the heavenly abode of their kingdom. The first stanza enquired about the road communications, villages, towns and cities of the world of soul through which they arrived just after physical death. The second stanza questions that, full of tears in the eye, lamenting because of extreme joy, did forefathers and mothers came to received you? The Third stanza: Are you cultivating crops in the field and eat food like us? Is there sun raises from east and set in the west? In the forth stanza enquired about the picturesque, topography, natural scenic beauty and flora & fauna of the death world. In fifth stanza poet expressing his own grief faced after departing with soul, telling that he was even unable to put his footsteps on proper place. The last stanza convincing the soul to return the real world like water cycle goes high up in the sky again and again.

WANCHO MODERN SONGS

Single- ꞏꞏꞏꞏꞏ ꞏꞏꞏꞏ ꞏꞏ . . . 🎵

Group- ꞏꞏ ꞏꞏ ꞏꞏꞏꞏꞏ, ꞏꞏ ꞏꞏ ꞏꞏꞏꞏꞏ, ꞏꞏꞏꞏꞏ ꞏꞏꞏꞏꞏ.

S- ꞏꞏꞏꞏꞏ ꞏꞏꞏꞏ ꞏꞏ ꞏꞏꞏꞏꞏ ꞏꞏ.

G- ꞏꞏ ꞏꞏ ꞏꞏꞏꞏꞏ, ꞏꞏ ꞏꞏ ꞏꞏꞏꞏꞏ, ꞏꞏꞏꞏꞏ ꞏꞏꞏꞏꞏ.

S- ꞏꞏꞏꞏꞏ ꞏꞏꞏꞏ ꞏꞏ ꞏꞏꞏꞏꞏꞏꞏ ꞏꞏꞏꞏ ꞏꞏꞏꞏꞏꞏ.

(2 times)

G- ꞏꞏꞏꞏꞏ ꞏꞏꞏꞏ ꞏꞏꞏꞏꞏ. (2 times)

S- ꞏꞏꞏꞏꞏ ꞏꞏꞏꞏ ꞏꞏ ꞏꞏꞏꞏꞏ ꞏꞏ.

   S- ꞏꞏꞏ ꞏꞏꞏꞏ ꞏꞏꞏ ꞏꞏꞏ,

   G- ꞏꞏ ꞏꞏ ꞏꞏꞏꞏꞏ ꞏꞏꞏꞏꞏ –ꞏꞏ.

   S- ꞏꞏꞏ ꞏꞏꞏ ꞏꞏꞏꞏꞏ ꞏꞏ ꞏꞏ,

   G- ꞏꞏꞏꞏ ꞏꞏꞏꞏꞏ ꞏꞏꞏꞏꞏ ꞏꞏꞏ.

   S- ꞏꞏꞏꞏ ꞏꞏꞏꞏ ꞏꞏ ꞏꞏ ꞏꞏꞏꞏꞏ,

   G- ꞏꞏ ꞏꞏ ꞏꞏ ꞏꞏ ꞏꞏ ꞏꞏꞏ.

   S- ꞏꞏꞏꞏꞏ ꞏꞏꞏꞏ, ꞏꞏꞏ ꞏꞏ ꞏꞏꞏꞏꞏ,

   G- ꞏꞏꞏꞏ ꞏꞏ ꞏꞏꞏꞏꞏ ꞏꞏꞏ ꞏꞏꞏ.

   S- ꞏꞏꞏꞏꞏ ꞏꞏꞏꞏ ꞏꞏꞏꞏꞏ ꞏꞏꞏꞏ.

   G- ꞏꞏꞏ ꞏꞏ ꞏꞏꞏꞏꞏ ꞏꞏꞏꞏꞏ.

   G- ꞏꞏ–ꞏ ꞏꞏꞏ ꞏꞏ ꞏꞏꞏ, ꞏꞏ–ꞏ ꞏꞏꞏ ꞏꞏ ꞏꞏꞏ.

   G- ꞏꞏ ꞏꞏ ꞏꞏꞏꞏꞏ, ꞏꞏ ꞏꞏ ꞏꞏꞏꞏꞏ, ꞏꞏꞏꞏꞏ ꞏꞏꞏꞏꞏ.

S- ꞏꞏꞏꞏꞏ ꞏꞏꞏꞏ ꞏꞏ ꞏꞏꞏꞏꞏꞏ ꞏꞏꞏꞏ ꞏꞏꞏꞏꞏꞏ.(2 times)

G- ꞏꞏꞏꞏꞏ ꞏꞏꞏꞏ ꞏꞏꞏꞏꞏ. (2 times)

S- ꞏꞏꞏꞏꞏ ꞏꞏꞏꞏ ꞏꞏ ꞏꞏꞏꞏꞏ ꞏꞏ.

   S- ꞏꞏꞏꞏ ꞏꞏꞏꞏ ꞏꞏꞏꞏ ꞏꞏꞏꞏ.

   G- ꞏꞏꞏꞏ ꞏꞏꞏꞏ ꞏꞏꞏꞏꞏ ꞏꞏꞏ,

   S- ꞏꞏꞏꞏꞏꞏ ꞏꞏꞏꞏꞏ, ꞏꞏꞏꞏꞏ ꞏꞏꞏꞏꞏ,

   G- ꞏꞏꞏꞏ ꞏꞏꞏꞏꞏ ꞏꞏꞏ.

   S- ꞏꞏꞏꞏꞏ ꞏꞏꞏꞏꞏ, ꞏꞏꞏꞏꞏ ꞏꞏꞏꞏꞏ,

   G- ꞏꞏꞏꞏ ꞏꞏꞏꞏ ꞏꞏꞏ ꞏꞏ.

   S- ꞏꞏ–ꞏꞏ ꞏꞏꞏꞏꞏ, ꞏꞏ–ꞏꞏ ꞏꞏꞏꞏꞏ,

   G- ꞏꞏꞏꞏꞏ, ꞏꞏꞏꞏꞏ, ꞏꞏꞏꞏꞏ ꞏꞏꞏ.

   S- ꞏꞏꞏꞏ ꞏꞏꞏꞏꞏ, ꞏꞏꞏꞏ ꞏꞏꞏꞏ,

   G- ꞏꞏꞏꞏꞏ ꞏꞏꞏ ꞏꞏꞏ ꞏꞏꞏꞏꞏ.

G- ꞏꞏꞏꞏꞏ ꞏꞏꞏꞏꞏ ꞏꞏꞏꞏꞏꞏ, ꞏꞏꞏꞏꞏ ꞏꞏꞏꞏꞏ ꞏꞏꞏꞏꞏ.

G- ꞏꞏ ꞏꞏ ꞏꞏꞏꞏꞏ, ꞏꞏ ꞏꞏ ꞏꞏꞏꞏꞏ, ꞏꞏꞏꞏꞏ ꞏꞏꞏꞏꞏ.

S-

(Repeat-4times)

   ꞏꞏꞏꞏꞏ ꞏꞏꞏꞏ ꞏꞏ ꞏꞏꞏ ꞏꞏꞏ ꞏꞏ.

(Repeat 4 times) together

WANCHO MODERN SONGS

Single : Aunok auga ley...
Group: Ku nang Wancho, Nang nang Wancho, Kem nang Wancho.
S: Aunok auga ley tha keh jo.
G: Ku nang Wancho, Nang nang Wancho, Kem nang Wancho.
S: Natuk Khaugo ma ganlahjo dingdan danggan ma. (2 times)
G: Pang nok gangphang nu ja-ye. (2 times)
S: Aunok auga ley tha keh jo.

    S: Apu apa aju ajong,
    G: Ma bang Wancho, Wancho-a.
    S: Hah ban gangjan jakah manney,
    G: Bangpu Wancho, Wancho kem.
    S: Tangnu Sangnu manney gangnih,
    G: Bangpu gam chi gang chau le.
    S: Pangnan Ja pha, lennu gangtan,
    G: Taipu Wancho Kom aga.
    S: Nyek to haphen, ngaito hasen.
    G: Lennu gangtan apongpu.
    G: Tik-e lum an bachu, Sung-e len an bachu.
    G: Ku nang Wancho, Nang nang Wancho, Kem nang Wancho.
S: Natuk Khaugo ma ganlahjo dingdan danggan ma. (2 times)
G: Pang nok gangphang nu ja-ye. (2 times)
S: Aunok auga ley tha keh jo.

    S: Gang pho puto pangpo Oriah.
    G: Pong lang la toak Wancho kem,
    S: Mai lang gan lang, phau kap soilau,
    G: Bang pu kosu kosa kem.
    S: Kahtok gimju, sah hi kakai,
    G: Le kap le sah le jing bang.
    S: Pu-e Wancho, Pa-e Wancho,
    G: Wancho, Wancho, Kah kha ma.
    S: Tik phai pan bang, sung phai go bang,
    G: Wancho ato mann lah tong.
G: Jumba hanyai loi pong gong, toak ba hasun sonu long.
G: Ku nang Wancho, Nang nang Wancho, Kem nang Wancho.

                                         (Repeat–4times)
S: Aunok auga ley tha keh jo.   (Repeat–4times) together

WANCHO MODERN SONGS

Translated into English

Single: Which caste, tribe or habitation.....
Group: I am a Wancho, You are a Wancho, We are Wanchos.

S: Do not inquire about caste, tribe or habitation.

G: I am a Wancho, You are a Wancho, We are Wanchos.

G: Recognize through ear-hole, hairstyle and lingo.

G: By the nation of the universe.
S: Do not inquire about caste, tribe or habitation.

S: Sine the day of Aju, Ajong,
G: Existing, Wancho, Wancho-a:
S: Since the day of division,
G: We are known as Wancho, Wancho.
S: Since arrival from Tangnu, Sangnu,
G: We follow ritual ceremonies.
S: The Sun and the Moon which illuminates the universe,
G: Are having with the Wancho.
S: Neither fails at night, nor withers in day,
G: The Sun and the Moon are as it is.
G: Even if foreign influences overtake Wancho,
G: I am a Wancho, You are a Wancho, We are Wanschos.

G: Recognize through ear-hole, hairstyle and lingo.

G: By the nation of the universe.
S: Do not inquire about caste, tribe or habitation.

S: Celebrates Oriah festival every year.
G: Sacrificing animals, we the Wanchos,
S: With great achievements, Prosperity and bestow it,
G: We are the descendants of them.
S: Cultivates and harvest crops,
G: Devour it since primordial.
S: Grandfather was Wancho, father is also Wancho,
G: Wancho, Wancho, on the earth.
S: Compete in every sphere with the rest of human race,
G: This is the identity of Wancho.

G: Neither soften buffalo's horn on boiling, nor burnt iver's stone into ashes.

G: Similarly to that, I am a Wancho, You are a Wancho, We are Wanchos.   (Repeated 4 times)

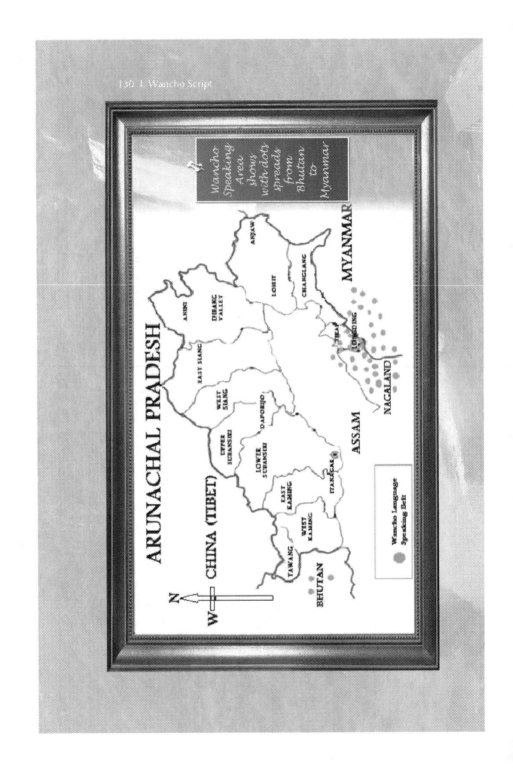

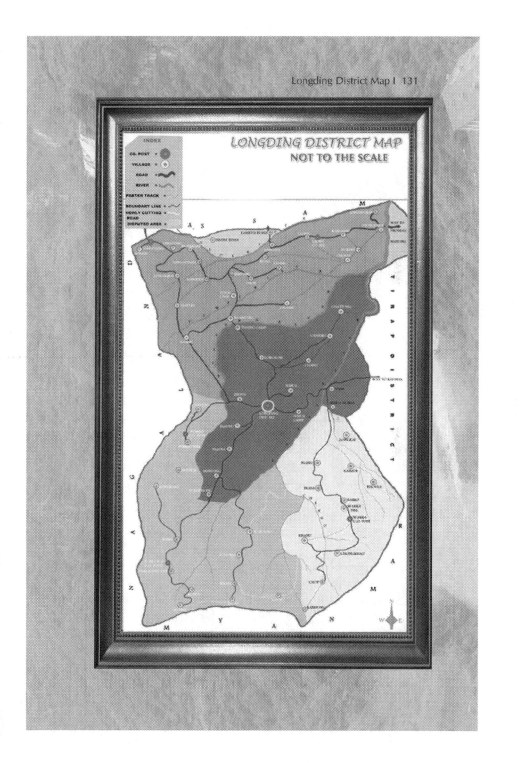

18 Significance of LOGO

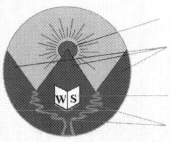

The sun symbolised an power and rich culture of the Wancho Society

The mountain ranges symbolised an English letter "W" which comes at first place while writing 'WANCHO'.

Book (WS) contained Wancho Script

The two rivers flowing from valleys of the the mountain range signifies the river 'TISSING and TISSA'

This LOGO has been designed for the symbol of Wancho Script and related works in the future. Morphologically, the sun is rising behind the mountain range with a garland forming tree like structure and W, S in the middle space. In the deepest sense, the sun symbolized the supreme power of the world as well as Wancho valley which is compared with the rich culture of the Wancho Society. The mountain range covered with evergreen flora and fauna spread to wide horizons from East to West shows the popularity of the Wancho as "W" which comes at the first place while writing a word 'WANCHO'. In the middle there is a symbol of book having Wancho Script (WS) containing unexplored virgin knowledge of Wancho. The garland like blue colour oozing/flowing from the valleys of mountain range is the river TISSING and TISSA.

WANCHO YOUTHS BEATING THE LOGDRUM

19 KINSHIP TERMS IN WANCHO

1. Maternal Grandfather
2. Maternal Grandmother
3. Grandfather
4. Grandmother
5. Father — (including all clan of father's age)
6. Mother
7. Elder brother
8. Younger brother — (address in their name)
9. Elder brother's wife — (by name if she is younger)
10. Younger brother's wife — by name (in case she is elder- etc.)
11. Maternal uncle (eldest)
12. Maternal uncle (younger)
13. Mother's elder brother's wife
14. Mother's younger brother's wife
15. Mother's brother's daughter — by name/
16. Father's elder sister
17. Father's younger sister
18. Father's elder brother's wife
19. Father's younger brother's wife
20. Wife's elder brother
21. Wife's younger brother — by name (if elder than you)
22. Step mother
23. Father's elder brother
24. Father's younger brother
25. Elder brother
26. Younger brother — by name
27. Husband — by name or Khoi or nick name

28. Wife   "   "   "   "

29. Father's elder sister's husband

           𞋃𞋃/𞋃𞋃/𞋃𞋃

30. Father's younger sister's husband

           𞋃𞋃/𞋃𞋃/𞋃𞋃

31𞋃.Father's sister's daughter   by name/𞋃𞋃/𞋃𞋃

32. Father's sister's son   by name/𞋃𞋃/𞋃𞋃/𞋃𞋃/
                                     𞋃𞋃/𞋃𞋃/𞋃𞋃

33. Elder sister   Nyathong/Jalong/Nachong

34. Younger sister   by name

35. Elder sister's husband   𞋃𞋃𞋃/𞋃𞋃𞋃/𞋃𞋃/
                                     𞋃𞋃𞋃| 𞋃𞋃𞋃𞋃𞋃

36. Younger sister's husband   by name (if younger)/𞋃𞋃𞋃/
                                     𞋃𞋃𞋃𞋃/𞋃𞋃𞋃

37. Wife's father   𞋃𞋃/𞋃𞋃/depending upon
                         the relationship/𞋃𞋃/𞋃𞋃

38. Wife's mother   𞋃𞋃/𞋃𞋃/𞋃𞋃

39. Husband's father   𞋃𞋃𞋃/𞋃𞋃/𞋃𞋃

40. Husband's mother   𞋃𞋃/𞋃𞋃/𞋃𞋃

41. Wife's elder brother's wife   𞋃𞋃𞋃/𞋃𞋃/𞋃𞋃

42. Wife's younger brother's wife   by name/𞋃𞋃𞋃

43. Daughter in law   by name/𞋃𞋃𞋃

In Wancho Community there are two major clans (Jan); (1) Wangham/Chief, (2) Wangpan/Pansa/Commoners. Wangham Clan and Wangpan/Pansa Clan are opposite to each other, marriage can take place with opposite clans, but it is strictly prohibited within the same clan in a village/society. In case of Wangham, socially legitimate provision is given to marry Chief's daughter of other village, only their offspring shall be the next Chief of that village. For the commoners too, it has been legalized in some villages that, inter-villages' marriage (From different village) can be practiced without prohibition in Wangsa-Wangsa marriage and Wangpan-Wangpan marriage depending upon the social acceptance.

20 MY MESSAGE TO THE PEOPLE

Dear Friends,

I cannot write well but my extreme LOVE and AFFECTION to you forced me to write this few words. Apart from the subject topic concerned, I would like to quote few lines of my personal view on the principle of life. Life is full of sorrow if we are unable to understand it; very beautiful and very wonderful if we are able to understand it. We prefer to live a happy life. To live a happy life we should remember the three rules. These are:

(i) **BIRTH:** When we took birth, we cried due to unbearable and uncontrollable pain.

(ii) **LIFE:** Since birth we find that seems everything is going against us till now.

(iii) **DEAD:** When we die, we will cry because of grasping/ pinching pain.

Pain and suffering, along with joy & happiness, are the natural laws of life. As we have been assigned sufferings since our conception in mother's wombs, we must be ready to continue facing it up to the tomb. It is the real meaning of life. Let us suffer for truth and for the good. Because "In every action there is equal and opposite reaction", according to Newton's Law. Similarly, "In every good and bad action there is equal and opposite reaction".

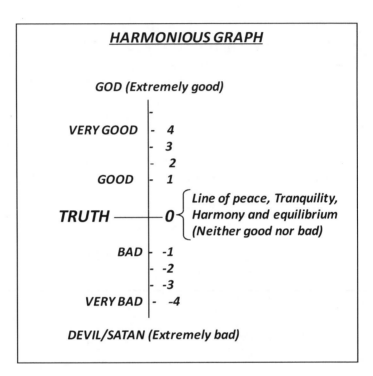

This graph shows that TRUTH lies on the origin where there are peace, tranquility, equilibrium and social harmony; it is neither good nor bad. Good extends towards god so good is god and bad extends towards devil/Satan so bad is Satan. God is not good for Satan/devil and Satan is not good for god. Both are opposite to each other, but both originated from the 'TRUTH'. Therefore, neither bad defeats nor good wins TRUTH always wins.

Knowing the fact, let us be simple & genuine so that the balance, equilibrium, tranquility, peace, and social harmony of humanity is maintained. To follow these, first we should know the universal truth what Vedanta taught us, which is hidden in our culture.

To bring the lost culture it is important to know the following comparison.

Internal Requirements	External Requirements
Brain	Knowledge
Nerve	Education
Blood	Book
Muscles	Work
Bones	Natural Resources

External requirements can be made available only if there are no crisis/disturbances in the Internal Requirement. But unfortunately, our internal requirements are facing a crises if my observation and research is not wrong. Now we need to reform or repair our damaged body parts by leaving drugs like opium, tobaccos, etc. One should stop drinking and indulging in social taboos, evil and dirty activities.

Nature has given everything in proportion according to our needs/requirements in the form of natural bio-chemistry and we must be contended with that. But today our planet is suffering because of artificial chemistry used in wrong way. My request to you is to "Live Naturally with Nature" and my motto of invention of script is to preserve our hidden truth and richness of culture through writing.

Being a Wancho, I must share with you the responsibilities to work for the preservation of our culture, nature and the humanity in the world. Wanchos of new born District Longding have always been known for their creative art, hard work, and peace loving nature since the time immemorial.

But, today these words seems 'word of mouth' because of the increase of opium addiction among the youths and of alcoholic teenagers. Our ancestors were winded with moral fiber and true nature. We are the descendants of them. Therefore we must possess their character/genes in our DNA and blood. Let us exercise to bring it back. By virtue of natural selection, we are settled in such a place where there is moderate temperature, sufficent rainfall, large topography, and plenty of flora and fauna lighted up by the sun rays from the hilly horizons covered with natural scenic beauty. Seeing these, our minds should be filled with joy & hope, not with a desire for drugs. Our soil is favorable almost for every vegetations. Let us divert our mind towards green revolution.

Therefore, old fashioned Jhum Cultivation can be replaced by modern commercial farmings like tea gardening, Paan (Betel leave) cultivation, Rubber plantation, Orange plantation, Cardamom cultivation, etc. instead of opium cultivation. "Soil is gold, time is money and you are makers". It is fortunate to have our area declared as a new district. So, let us work with a new energy, new hope, and a new vision towards a new civilization. Never forget that, every developed nation sustained on hard work, sincerity and honesty. Why can't we?

B. Losu

21 GLOSSARY

Affricate	A speech sound that is made up of a plosive followed immediately by a fricative.
Ajong	The first female on earth (Adam).
Aju	The first male on earth (Eve).
Ancestor	A person in a family who lived a long time ago.
Anthropology	The study of the human race, especially of its origins, development, customs and beliefs.
Apu	The father of your father or mother (Grandfather).
Articulation	The expression of an idea or a feeling in words.
Aspiration	A strong desire to have or do.
Authentic	Known to be real and genuine and not a copy.
Aver	To state firmly and strongly saying that is true.
Chahnu/Thahnu	A large wild animal of the cat family that has yellowish fur with black lines (Tiger).
Civilization	A state of human society that is very developed and organized.
Classification	The act or process of putting people or things into a group or class.
Communication	The activity or process of expressing ideas and feelings or of giving people information.
Complex	Made of many different things or parts that are connected; difficult to understand.

Confine	To keep inside the limits of a particular activity, subject, area, etc.
Consonant	A speech sound made by completely or partly stopping the flow of air being breathed out through the mouth.
Contextualize	To consider in relation to the situation in which it happens or exists.
Conventional	Tending to follow what is done or considered, acceptable by society in general; normal and ordinary, and perhaps not very interesting.
Conversation	An informal talks involving a small group of people or only two; the activity of talking in this way.
Culture	The customs and beliefs, art, way of life and social organization of a particular country or group.
Devnagri	The alphabet used to write Sanskrit, Hindi and some other Indian languages.
Encyclopaedia	A book or set of books giving information about all areas of knowledge or about different areas of one particular subject, usually arranged in alphabetical order.
Endanger	To put in a situation in which they could be harmed or damaged.
Ethnic	Connected with or belonging to a nation, race or a person that shares a cultural tradition.
Fascinating	Extremely interesting and attractive.
Fhagong	A tall plant grown for its large yellow grains that are used for making flour or eaten as a vegetable (Maize).
Fricative	A speech sound made by forcing breath out through a narrow space in the mouth with the lips, teeth or tongue in particular position.

Friction	The action of one objects or surface moving against another.
Gee	A thin string of cotton, wool, silk, etc. used for sewing or making cloth (Thread in English).
Glottal Stops	A speech sound made by closing and opening the glottis, which in English some-time takes the place /t/ as in butter.
Harmonious	Friendly, peaceful and without any disagreement.
Hing	The study and treatment of diseases and injuries (Medicine).
Horizon	The furthest that you can see, where the sky seems to meet the land or the sea.
Hot/Ton	A common fly that lives in houses (House-fly).
Hum	The house or flat/apartment that you live in, especially with family (Home).
Immemorial	That has existed for longer than people can remember.
Incantation	Special words that are spoken or sung to have a magic effect; the act of speaking or singing these words.
Indigenous	Belonging to a particular place rather than coming to it from somewhere else (Native).
Inspiration	The process that takes place when you sees or hears that causes to have exciting new ideas or makes to create, especially in art, music or literature.
Invention	A thing or an idea that has been invented.
Jan/Zan	A chemical element, hard strong metal that is used to make steel and is also

	found in small quantities in blood and food (Iron).
Khohom	A covering made to fit the head (Hat) or headgear.
Ki /Hee	An animal with four legs and a tail often kept as a pet or trained for work, for example hunting or guarding home (Dog).
Letnu /Lennu	The round object that moves around the earth once every 27 ½ days and shines at night by light reflected from the sun (Moon).
Linguistic	Connected with language or the scientific study of language.
Logicians	A person who studies or is skilled in logic.
Loi	A large animal of the cow family which has curved horns (Buffalo).
Long	A hard solid mineral substance that is found in the ground (Stone).
Maihu/Maidu	A large four footed animal having horns and tail kept on farms to produce milk or beef (Cow).
Meditation	The practice of thinking deeply in silence, especially for religious reasons or in order to make your mind calm.
Mia	A small animal with soft fur that people often keep as a pet that catch and kill birds and mice (Cat).
Mik	Either of the two organs on the face that you see with (Eye).
Mongtam	The organ in the chest that pumps/sends blood around the body through veins, it is usually on the left side in the humans (Heart).

Moral	Concerned with principles of right and wrong behaviour.
Na	Either of the organs on the sides of the head that you hear with (Ear).
Natural	Existing in nature; not made or caused by humans.
Ngun	What you earn by working or selling things, and use to buy things (Money).
Niah	A creature that lives in water, breathes through gills, and uses fins and a tail for swimming (Fish).
Nucleus	The central part of an atom, consisting only of protons and neutrons held together by the strong force.
Nyem	A large reptile with a long tail, hard skin and very big jaws that lives in rivers and lakes in hot countries (Crocodile).
Omnipresent	Present everywhere.
Organization	A group of people who form a business, club, etc. together in order to achieve a particular aim.
Organs	A part of body that has a particular purpose, such as the heart or the brain; part of a plant with a particular purpose.
Pedagogic	Concerning teaching learning methods.
Philosopher	A person who studies or writes about philosophy.
Phonetics	The study of speech sounds and how they are produced.
Phonology	The speech sounds of a particular language; the study of these sounds.
Phu	An object with a round folding frame of long straight pieces of metal covered with material that you use to protect yourself from rain or from hot sun (Umbrella).

Plagiarize   To copy another person's ideas, words or work and pretend that they are your own.

Plosive   A speech sound made by stopping the flow of air coming out of the mouth and then suddenly releasing it.

Preservation   The act of keeping in its original state or in good condition.

Pronunciation   The way in which a language or a particular word or sound is pronounced.

Psychologist   A scientist who studies and is trained in psychology.

Pu   A reptile with a very long thin body and no legs, having poisonous venom in its fangs (Snake).

Rehearsal   Time that is spent practising a play or piece of music in preparation for a public performance.

22 BIBLIOGRAPHY

Books	Authors
Linguistics & Phonetics	Late Dr. Radhey L. Varshney M.A.,Ph.D.C.T.E. (C.I.E.F.L) Ex. Prof.& Head. P.G. & Research Deptt. Of English University, Gurukul Kangri. Published by Student Store, 35-A, Civil Lines, Rampur Bagh, Bareilly-2510102
Revised by	Dr. S.N. Arora M.A., Ph.D., D. Litt. Published by Student Store 35 A-1, Civil lines, Rampur Bagh, Bareilly. Sixteenth Edition; 2005-06
Selected Poems & Stories	Edited by Dr. M.Q. Khan
Classification of Languages	Shafer, Benedict Egerod and Voegelin.

Some Pictures has been taken from Children's Big Book of Questions and Answers (Encyclopedia); Pictures from page-23 is own created; Page-111: Population Data collected, based on Population Census of India 2001. Page-26,27: Stephen Hawking, Professor of Mathematics in Cambridge University who wrote the inspiring sequel to A Brief History of Time and winner of the 2002 Aventis Prizes for Science Books. Ref. Linguistics & Phonetics, Sixteenth Edition-2005-06. for Pages-24-26, 65-85. Wancho Modern Song composed by Mr. Nawki Ngandam. Human Body, Image collection assisted by Mr. Jatwang Wangsa. Art by Mr. Manlem Losu. Symbol: www.*Wikipadia.com*; Names of Days, week, month & Year: Ref: Mr. Phawang Wangham of K/Noknu village. Longding District Map : Mr. Kingwang Wangham.

ABOUT THE AUTHOR

Banwang Losu, born in the village of Kamhua Noknu, graduated from Dera Natung Government College, Itanagar, in the year 2006.

Presently, he is a teacher in Longding District, Arunachal Pradesh (India).